D0820821

Companioning the Bereaved

Companioning the Bereaved

A Soulful Guide for Caregivers

Alan D. Wolfelt, Ph.D.

Companion Press is an imprint of the Center for Loss and Life Transition, 3735 Broken Bow Road, Fort Collins, Colorado 80526, (970) 226-6050, www.centerforloss.com.

Companion Press books may be purchased in bulk for sales promotions, premiums and fundraisers. Please contact the publisher at the above address for more information.

Printed in the United States of America.

15 14 13 12 11 10 09 08 07 06   5 4 3 2 1

ISBN 1-879651-41-6

To the thousands of mourners over the last three decades who have accepted my hospitality and allowed me the privilege of companioning them in their grief. The precious lessons you have taught me I now humbly pass on to others.

Companion Press is dedicated to the education and support of both the bereaved and bereavement caregivers. We believe that those who companion the bereaved by walking with them as they journey in grief have a wondrous opportunity: to help others embrace and grow through grief—and to lead fuller, more deeply-lived lives themselves because of this important ministry.

For a complete catalog and ordering information,
write or call or visit our website:

Companion
P R E S S

Companion Press
The Center for Loss and Life Transition
3735 Broken Bow Road
Fort Collins, CO 80526
(970) 226-6050
FAX 1-800-922-6051
wolfelt@centerforloss.com
www.centerforloss.com

Contents

Part One

A Soulful Philosophy of Grief Care:
The Art of Companioning
the Bereaved

"It's not surprising that as our culture advances in information and technology, we seem to become more inarticulate about matters of the heart. We quantify 'human behavior' and develop programs of therapy and treatment, and yet the procrustean trimming of the soul to fit our programs of science doesn't have much effect. We still encounter the soul briefly, as a set of problems, rather than as a creative and constructive source of life."—Thomas Moore

Introduction:
A Declaration of My Intent

At the very heart of grief lies an irreducible mystery. I have come to discover that grief is a dimension of life experience that cannot be approached through rational thought. Instead, it responds more appropriately to humbled souls. In this spirit, I invite you to open your heart to what follows.

My tenets of "companioning" the bereaved were written several years ago as I sat in a gazebo on the sacred grounds of the Center for Loss and Life Transition. Since that time of grace in my life, which encouraged me to try to express in words what I do when I "companion" people in grief, I've been honored that many people have encouraged me to teach more about these tenets. I've written the following words with a humbled heart and a desire to help people help others during time of grief and loss.

This particular book has been long in coming; however, for that I take great pride. Many of my colleagues and students have urged me to write this book for some time. Yet, I felt a need to wait, listen and learn before I could express in words the art of companioning people in grief. It was important to me that I write this book in a manner and tone congruent with the ideas I am trying to communicate. I found I had to wait for my thoughts to coalesce in ways that would allow me to teach about my beliefs and how I try to "be" in my effort to help others come out of the darkness of their grief and into the light of living until they die. I believe this waiting was a part of my own maturation process.

I am very honored that there is now an international network of thousands of people who have trained with me surrounding the companioning philosophy of caregiving to people in grief. Yet, there seems to be a place for this book in that many of my colleagues have either had to imagine, question, project, and, honestly, at times even judge what I do. In part this book is a "coming out of the closet" as a "responsible rebel."

Responsible Rebel: One who questions assumptive models surrounding grief and loss and challenges those very models. Rebels are not afraid to question established structures and forms. At the same time, rebels respect the rights of others to use different models of understanding, and provide leadership in ways that empower people rather than diminish them. So, if the contents of this book resonate with you, please join me in being a responsible rebel!

In sum, my deep hope is that this resource will serve as a source of encouragement and help to those who want to learn more about the art of companioning people in grief. My experience suggests that few helping situations are more challenging—or more rewarding—than the opportunity to assist people impacted by loss in their lives. Perhaps through deepening our human capacity to respond to each other in times of grief we can continue to enrich each moment of our living.

Why A "Soulful" Guide?

When people have come to me for support in grief, the soul is present. When they try as best they can to wrap words around their grief, trusting me with their vulnerability, I know we are meeting at a soul level. To look into the eyes of someone mourning the death of someone precious is to look into the window of the soul.

Their willingness to allow me to walk with and learn from them has been an education of the heart and soul. "Soul" is discovered in the quality of what I'm experiencing when I'm honored to be present to them. If my intent is anchored in truth and integrity, if they are discovering a reason to go on living (redefining their worldview and searching for meaning), then they are rich in soul, and so am I. Therefore, for me, companioning another human being in grief means giving attention to those experiences that give my life, and the lives of those I attempt to help, a richness and depth of meaning.

Soul really has to do with a sense of the heart being touched by feelings. An open heart that is grieving is a "well of reception;" it is moved entirely by what it has perceived. Soul also has to do with the overall journey of life as a story, as a representation of deep inner meaning. Soul is not a thing, but a dimension of experiencing life and living. I see soul as the primary essence of our true nature, our spirit self, or our life force.

Being soulful as it relates to companioning people in grief is, in part, to acknowledge a need for people to have "safe places" to authentically mourn. Then, in order to respond to that need, it is to go within yourself and nurture and develop your soul in ways that give expression to your compassion. My hope is that this book helps you do just that!

Grief is Not an Illness:
Inappropriate Assumptions Surrounding Our Modern Understanding of Grief and Loss

As a teenager who had come to experience my own life losses, I set out to discover the principles that help bereaved people heal in grief. I hoped to communicate those principles to anyone interested in honoring my story. To my dismay, I discovered that the majority of caregiving models for grief counselors were intertwined with the medical model of mental health care.

For many caregivers, grief in contemporary society has been medicalized and perceived as if it is an illness that with proper assessment, diagnosis, and treatment can be cured. This paradigm dictates that we as caregivers, having studied and absorbed a body of knowledge and become experts, are responsible for "curing" our patients. How arrogant!

The language we use to describe the practice of grief support exposes our attitudes and beliefs about counseling as well as determines our practices. Because numerous historical roots of psychotherapy are deeply grounded in a medical model, because the medical model appears more scientific than other alternatives, and because the economics of practice are interfaced in a healthcare delivery system, the natural tendency has been to adopt medical model language.

As I explored the words used in counseling the bereaved, I was taken aback: symptoms of pathology; disorders; diagnosis; and treatments. In my own search to learn so I could teach, I found that these more clinical, medical model approaches have limitations that are profound and far-reaching.

I discovered that our modern understanding of grief all too often projects that for "successful" mourning to take place, the person must "disengage from the deceased" and, by all means "let go." We even have all sorts of books full of techniques on how to help others "let go" or reach "closure."

At bottom, I discovered that our current models desperately needed what we could refer to as a "supplement of the soul." It seemed glaringly obvious to me that as fellow travelers in the journey into grief, we needed more life-giving, hope-filled models that incorporated not only the mind and body, but the soul and the spirit! I found myself resonating more with the writings of people like Ram Das, Stephen Levine, Victor Frankl, James Hillman, Thomas Moore and Carl Jung.

Actually it was Carl Jung's writing that helped me understand that every psychological struggle is ultimately a matter of spirituality. In the end, as we as human beings mourn, we must discover meaning to go on living our tomorrows without the physical presence of someone we have loved. Death and grief are spiritual journeys of the heart and soul.

Yet, our modern Western culture's understanding of grief often urges mourners to deny any form of continued relationship with the person who died. For many mental health caregivers, the hallmark of so-called "pathology" has been rooted in terms of sustaining a relationship to the dead. In reality, the mourner actively shifts the relationship from one of presence to one of memory. Or, as the playwright Robert Anderson wisely noted, "Death ends a life; it does not end a relationship." In contrast, many other cultures throughout history have encouraged ongoing, interdependent relationships in some form after death. Beyond this recognition of a continued relationship of memory, most cultures provide bereaved people with rituals to encourage an appropriate relationship of memory, such as Mexico's "Day of the Dead."

Our modern understanding of grief all to often conveys that the end result of bereavement is a series of completed tasks, extinguished pain, and the establishment of new relationships. I discovered that many mental health caregivers, in attempting to make a science of grief, had compartmentalized complex emotions with neat clinical labels.

Our modern understanding of grief all too often uses a "recovery" or "resolution" definition to suggest a return to "normalcy." Recovery, as understood by some mourners and caregivers alike, is erroneously seen as an absolute, a perfect state of reestablishment. We seem to want to go around any so-called "negative" moods and emotions quickly and efficiently. Yet, it occurred to me that if our role as caregivers is to first observe the soul as it is, then we need to abolish what I call the "resolution wish."

Our modern understanding of grief for some is based on the model of crisis theory that purports that a person's life is in a state of homeostatic balance, then something comes along (like the death of

⬦⬦⬦⬦⬦⬦⬦⬦⬦⬦⬦⬦⬦⬦⬦⬦⬦⬦⬦⬦⬦⬦⬦⬦⬦⬦⬦⬦⬦⬦⬦

"Negative" Emotions

The emotions of grief are often referred to as being "negative," as if they are inherently bad emotions to experience. This judgment feeds our culture's attitude that these emotions should be denied or "overcome." In reality, these care-eliciting emotions are what alerts companions to the reality that the mourner has special needs that call for support and comfort. Emotions are not bad or good. They just are.

⬦⬦⬦⬦⬦⬦⬦⬦⬦⬦⬦⬦⬦⬦⬦⬦⬦⬦⬦⬦⬦⬦⬦⬦⬦⬦⬦⬦⬦⬦⬦

someone loved) and knocks the person out of balance. Caregivers are taught intervention goals to reestablish the prior state of homeostasis and a return to "normal" functioning. There is only one major problem with this theory: it doesn't work. Why? Because a person's life is changed forever by the death of someone loved. We are transformed by grief and do not return to prior states of "normal" based on interventions by outside forces.

❖❖❖❖❖❖❖❖❖❖❖❖❖

The Resolution Wish

We wish that grief would resolve. We wish that it was linear and finite. We wish that we could wake up one day and our painful thoughts and feelings would all be "over." Grief never resolves, however. While we can learn to reconcile ourselves to it, grief is transformative and life-changing

❖❖❖❖❖❖❖❖❖❖❖❖❖

Our modern understanding of grief all too often "pathologizes" normal experiences. Traditional psychology has focused the majority of attention on the diagnosis and treatment of pathologies and in the quest for "fixes," little attention has been paid to the nature of emotional or spiritual health. As one author observed, "The exclusive focus on pathology that has dominated so much of our discipline results in a model of the human being lacking the positive features that make life worth living."

Our modern understanding of grief all too often privatizes grief as an isolated, individual experience. Mourning, by nature of its definition— "a shared social response to loss"—must be viewed in the broader context of social and family perspectives. In fact, the person often perceived as "not doing well" in grief is usually the one who is trying to get help for the family system.

In sum, I discovered in my twelve years of university-based training and in reading the available literature on grief counseling that our modern understanding of grief all too often lacks any appreciation for and attention to the spiritual, soul-based nature of the grief journey. As authors such as Frankl, Fromm, and Jung noted years ago (and Hillman and Moore more recently), academic psychology has been too interfaced with the natural sciences and laboratory methods of weighing, counting and objective reporting.

Some of us, often through no fault of our own, but perhaps by the contamination of our formal training, have overlooked the journey into grief as a soul-based journey. We need to think and reflect about grief care differently than we now do. Because while its mission in our society is certainly important, our current misunderstanding of its essence misinforms our capacity to reflect on it wisely.

This book seeks to undermine those practices that oppress grieving persons and families and provide interested people with food for reflective thought surrounding the importance of questioning the traditional medical model of mental health care. More important, the content presents an alternative model based on "companioning" versus "treating" one's fellow human beings in grief.

Critical self-observation would suggest that perhaps we rely too much on psychosocial, biological and psychodynamic constructs that we have been taught to "treat away," such as depression, anxiety, and loss of control. In our attempt to gain scientific credibility, we may have become our own worst enemies! In our attempt to be respected as part of established mental health care, we may be disrespecting the very people who need our compassionate care.

Without doubt, the grief journey requires contemplation and turning inward. In other words, it requires depression, anxiety and loss of control. It requires going to the wilderness. Quietness and emptiness invite the heart to observe signs of sacredness, to regain purpose, to rediscover love, to renew life! Searching for meaning, reasons to get one's feet out of bed, and understanding the pain of loss are not the domain of the medical model of bereavement care. Experience has taught me that it is the mysterious, spiritual dimension of grief that allows us to go on living until we, too, die.

Additional Influences Impacting the Care of Grievers

There are also a number of other cultural, technological and demographic trends that have converged in recent decades and have shaped our modern understanding of grief and grief care:

- **We live in the world's first death-free generation.**
  Many people now live into their 40s and 50s before they experience
  a close personal loss. Today two-thirds of all deaths in the U.S. each
  year happen to people 65 or older.

  In the early 1900s, on the other hand, most children had been to
  many funerals by the age of ten. (In 1900 over half of all deaths in
  the U.S. each year were deaths of children 15 or younger.) Aging, illness and death were an everyday part of family life. While we certainly appreciate the medical advances that have helped lower the
  mortality rate and prolong lifespans, they are also distancing us from
  aging, illness, death and grief.

- **We live in a fast-paced culture.**
  Have you also noticed how we like many things to be fast in our culture? It seems that efficiency or speed is often placed above effec-
  tiveness. But grief isn't fast, and it's not possible to "get over it."

- **We're disconnected from each other.**
  For starters, many people have lost a sense of community. Not long
  ago, people shared their lives with those around them. Generation
  after generation, families lived in the same town or at least the same
  state. Neighbors visited on the front porch, gathered for meals and
  took care of each other's children. People knew each other. People
  cared about each other. Now, like no other time in history, many
  people feel alone and unconnected to groups.

  One recent study found that 71 percent of Americans didn't know
  their neighbors. Adults and children alike live among strangers. The
  number of people who report they never spend time with their
  neighbors has doubled in only the last twenty years.

  We have evolved from a country of primary relationships to one of
  secondary relationships. Primary relationships are ones in which people know each other in a variety of roles—as friends, neighbors,
  coworkers. Secondary relationships are ones in which people are
  merely acquaintances. We may sit next to someone at work, but
  often we don't know much about him—where he lives, if he has a
  family, what his hobbies are.

As we have connected to the internet, we have disconnected from each other. Our state-of-the-art technology has created a new kind of person, one who is plugged into machines instead of fellow human beings. Some of us talk more via e-mail than we do to our own family members.

- **We value self-reliance.**

Have you noticed that the biggest section in bookstores these days is the self-help section? We live in an era of rugged individualism and independence. We reward people for "doing it on their own." How many of us grew up learning the North American motto, "If you want it done right, do it yourself"? Yet, when someone in your life dies, you must be interdependent and connected to the world around you if you are to heal. In short, rugged individualism and mourning don't mix well.

- **We have lost the symbolism of death.**

Philippe Ariès, in his book *The Hour of Our Death*, identifies the symbols representing death in art and in literature, as well as in funeral and burial customs. He maintains, and I agree, that symbols of death are no longer prominent in contemporary North American culture, and that gone with them is a link that in previous generations provided meaning and a sense of continuity for the living.

In generations past, for example, the bereaved used to wear mourning clothes or armbands, often black, that symbolized their sorrow. In some subcultures, mourners also hung wreaths on the door to let others know that someone loved had died. Today we can't even tell who the bereaved are. For some, memorial flowers, both at the funeral and at the cemetery, are becoming another ousted symbol. Today we opt for the more practical but less spiritual monetary donation: "In lieu of flowers, please send contributions to . . ."

Perhaps the ultimate symbol of death that we are tending more and more to forsake is the dead person's body. When viewed at the visitation or during the funeral service itself, the body encourages mourners to confront the reality and the finality of the death. Of course, opponents of viewing often describe it as unseemly, expensive, undignified and unnecessary. Yet, seeing and spending time with the body allows for last goodbyes and visual confirmation that someone loved is indeed dead. In generations past, the body often served as the very locus of mourning; the bereaved came to the dead person's home to view the body, pay their last respects and support the primary mourners. In fact, the body was often displayed for days before burial. Today, with our increasing reliance on closed caskets and direct cremation with no services, we are forgetting the importance of this tradition.

As Ariès writes, "The change (in death's role in our society) consists precisely in banishing from the sight of the public not only death but with it, its icon. Relegated to the secret, private space of the home or the anonymity of the hospital, death no longer makes any sign." As we eliminate the symbols of death, we also appear to be eliminating the rituals, historically rich in symbolism, that remind us of the death of others as well as our own mortality.

• **The deritualization of North American culture**. Beyond the loss of death symbols, the bigger issue is that we as a culture appear to be forgetting the importance of rituals surrounding life and death. Death rituals and ceremonies have been with us since the beginning of humankind. Those who have gone before us in this world—in fact, all of our predecessors—embraced both life and death in ceremony. Rituals were a central part of everyday life, whether it was acknowledging new life, sharing a meal together, celebrating the harvest or burying the dead. New life, loss of life and most every major life transition were met with ceremony.

Yet, in recent years, more and more North Americans are questioning the value of planning and participating in ceremonies that honor the "rites of passage" from life to death. There is an unfortunate perception that "educated" and "sophisticated" people are somehow above the need to openly express grief through public ceremony. A growing trend is to "dispose" of the dead and quickly return to "normal life." The problem is that if we don't acknowledge the significance of death, we don't acknowledge the significance of life!

• **We deny our own mortality.**
One woman once said to me, "I don't do death." She is not alone. Many people in North America today deny their own mortality. Author Paul Irion reflects that, "Man knows that he is only assuming

invulnerability, that he is ultimately vulnerable, and yet to admit this fact totally is to be defenseless." In other words, denying our own mortality is better than the alternative

Sigmund Freud also wrote of this theme in his *Collected Papers* when he concluded, "At bottom no one believes in his own death, or to put the same thing in another way, in the unconscious every one of us is convinced of his own immortality."

In summary, death and grief were a common part of our everyday lives in past generations. Now they are unfamiliar strangers we are ill-equipped to greet and entertain when, from time to time, they come knocking on our door.

Blessed Are Those Who Mourn Quickly: Managed Care and the Rapid "Resolution" of Grief

As many of you readers know from experience, managed care health plans have developed in recent years in response to the need of insurance providers to limit healthcare (including mental health) benefits. Utilization reviewers representing these various plans usually decide how many sessions counselors and clients will have together, then subsequently review the client's progress and decide whether or not to authorize more sessions. A 1999 survey discovered that 80 percent of practitioners felt that they had lost complete control over aspects of care that they as clinicians should control (e.g., type and length of care).

Among other things, managed care has us wrestling with issues such as confidentiality, paperwork volume and control over type and number of counseling sessions. However, it is the deeper implications of managed care that keep coming up in my conversations with the many grief counselors and therapists I meet at my workshops or from whom I receive phone calls.

I'm more than concerned about how contemporary mental health care responds to the needs of the bereaved under our present managed care system. Obviously, we as caregivers cannot see people two or three times and "resolve" their grief. While our so-called "advanced culture" would like to think humans can quickly and efficiently overcome grief, reality suggests otherwise. This popular short-term orientation to mental health care implies a rational and mechanistic understanding of what is actually a spiritual journey involving the heart and soul. As noted in the excellent text *The Heroic Client*, "The bottom line: the medical model of mental health prevails and is so much a part of professional discourse that we do not notice its insidious influence."

Through no fault of their own, the general public has also been contaminated by this model. Some will approach the counseling relationship and essentially say, "I want you to fix me. The faster, the better. Tell me what I can do to resolve my grief and I'll do it." Yet, to heal in grief one must turn inward, slow down, embrace pain, and seek and accept support. I continue to see people at my Center for Loss and Life Transition who essentially believe they have come to find ways to get rid of symptoms. "Help me get rid of these feeling of confusion, numbness and self-doubt," they seem to be asking. If I quickly moved to do what many in North American culture think I should do, I'd be taking normal grief and mourning symptoms away from people all day long. Instead, I try to "watch out for," "keep and honor," and nurture souls as they encounter the hard work of mourning.

Quick fixes may in fact achieve repression of normal symptoms of grief. But at what price? Repressed thoughts and feelings always return to haunt the human psyche. If we try to resist the overwhelming power of grief, it will inevitably express itself through fallout consequences such as difficulty in relationships, addictive behaviors, and chronic depression. I like to refer to these consequences as living in the "shadow of the ghosts" of grief (see page 31).

This current approach to mental health care is actually contributing to an epidemic of complicated morning in North America. Rather than allowing for the creation of safe places, or sanctuaries, where hurting people can mourn in doses when their heads and hearts are ready, this current model encourages people to deny their feelings. Pain and feelings of loss are seen as unnecessary and inappropriate. Yet, only in having the safety of people and places where we can move toward our wounds do we ultimately "reconcile," not resolve, death losses.

This current philosophy actually reinforces destructive societal messages such as, "carry on," "keep your chin up," and "keep busy." It's as if our current model of care shields its very self from acknowledging the human pain and loss, while not providing places for people to mourn.

Managed care has placed the focus on short-term, overt, measurable "progress" in grief. It's as if getting the person back to work is more important than restoring the soul. In my experience, many utilization reviewers from managed care companies advocate cognitive-behavioral therapy. A major problem with this is that we cannot help people heal in grief by simply thinking through the experience. As we have come to realize, in matters of life and death we must feel it to heal it. Managed care reinforces trying to "resolve" loss in one's head, not one's heart.

Sanctuary

A place of refuge from external demands. A space where the mourner is free to disengage from the outside world. A place where the need to turn inward and suspend will not be hurried or ridiculed.

The experience of integrating loss into the depths of one's soul does not take place in sound-bites. Healing doesn't occur in billable units of time. The human heart doesn't heal according to a time clock. When it comes to embracing grief, faster is certainly not better.

Caregivers cannot make instant rapport and safety like we make instant jello. What is often a critical ingredient to the integration of loss into one's life is the active empathy of another human being. To make claims that you can understand another human's raw grief too quickly is both a lie and an insult.

Of course, if grief were seen as a normal state of being (requiring long-term support and compassionate understanding) rather than as a disorder that needs to be eradicated, we could have even more problems. Why? Because at least now we can use the false language outlined in the *Diagnostic and Statistical Manual of Mental Disorders, Fourth Edition, APA 2000* called "Adjustment Disorder with Mixed Emotional Features" to procure reimbursement for a few sessions with grieving

"BRIEF" THERAPY: A GRIEF COUNSELING METHOD ~~FOR~~ MANAGED CARE...

HI. WHO DIED?
I'M SORRY! THERE, THERE.
TIME HEALS ALL WOUNDS.
TAKE CARE.

tic
tic
tic

1. "HI."

One of the shortest, friendliest words in our language. "Hi" develops instant rapport and acknowledges the mourner efficiently. (Avoid polysyllabic "Hellos" or "Good afternoons"; they consume too much time.)

4. "THERE, THERE."

A USEFUL PHRASE WHEN THE "I'M SO SORRY!" LINE ELICITS WEEPING. "THERE, THERE" DIPLOMATICALLY SAYS "AGAIN, I'M SORRY, BUT YOU DON'T HAVE TIME TO WASTE CRYING IN MY OFFICE, SO STOP."

2. "WHO DIED?"

THIS CLOSED-ENDED QUESTION GETS STRAIGHT TO THE POINT, ALLOWING THE MOURNER TO (QUICKLY) TELL HER STORY. ENCOURAGE THE MOURNER TO STRING TOGETHER ALL THE PERTINENT FACTS INTO ONE SENTENCE: "MY 42-YEAR-OLD HUSBAND OF 10 YEARS, FRED, DIED OF CANCER THREE MONTHS AGO, LEAVING ME TO CARE FOR OUR 6-YEAR-OLD SON JACK AND 8-YEAR-OLD DAUGHTER HANNAH." AVOID ASKING THE OPEN-ENDED "HOW ARE YOU?" – TALK ABOUT A PANDORA'S BOX OF THOUGHTS AND FEELINGS.

5. "TIME HEALS ALL WOUNDS."

This useful cliché promises the mourner that she will heal from this loss, giving her hope for the future. However, healing takes time and time is something the two of you don't have together, so move on to step 6.

3. "I'M SO SORRY!"

This phrase communicates empathy and concern. You are sorry, after all. Look meaningfully into the mourner's eyes as you say this and if you've done a good job of building rapport in your 5 minutes together, reach out and pat her hand.

6. "TAKE CARE."

A COMPASSIONATE YET FIRM CLOSER FOR THE SESSION. SOUNDS POLITE AND EMPATHETIC, BUT THIS PHRASE ALSO SUBTLY PUTS THE BURDEN OF HEALING BACK ON THE MOURNER, AS IN "YOU TAKE YOUR CARES AND WORK ON THEM ON YOUR OWN, BECAUSE WE'RE FINISHED HERE."

"BRIEF" THERAPY, as described above, is economical, efficient and healing therapy for mourners in the managed care setting. TOTAL SESSION TIME: 10 MINUTES.

people. (While some may question the ethics of this practice, it happens every day in counselors' offices across the U.S.) If, on the other hand, we were to make the mistake of giving a V-Code for "normal bereavement," we may well get a phone call or letter from the utilization reviewer stating "no sessions authorized."

We all are familiar with the Biblical beatitude, "Blessed are those who mourn, for they shall be comforted." The new managed care version might read, "Blessed are those who mourn quickly and efficiently in response to abbreviated counseling techniques, for they shall meet our criteria for successful treatment."

Foundations of "Companioning" One's Fellow Human Beings

I've always found it intriguing that the word "treat" comes from the Latin root word "tractare," which means "to drag." If we combine that with "patient," we can really get in trouble. "Patient" means "passive long-term sufferer," so if we treat patients, we drag passive, long-term sufferers. Simply stated, that's not very empowering .

On the other hand, the word "companion," when broken down into its original Latin roots, means "messmate": *com* for "with" and *pan* for "bread." Someone you would share a meal with, a friend, an equal. I have taken liberties with the noun "companion" and made it into the verb "companioning" because it so well captures the type of counseling relationship I support and advocate. That is the image of companioning—sitting at a table together, being present to one another, sharing, communing, abiding in the fellowship of hospitality.

Companioning the bereaved is not about assessing, analyzing, fixing or resolving another's grief. Instead, it is about being totally present to the mourner, even being a temporary guardian of her soul.

The companioning model is anchored in the "teach me" perspective. It is about learning and observing. In fact, the meaning of "observance" comes to us from ritual. It means not only to "watch out for" but also "to keep and honor," "to bear witness." The caregiver's awareness of this need to learn is the essence of true companioning.

If your desire is to support a fellow human in grief, you must create a "safe place" for people to embrace their feelings of profound loss. This safe place is a cleaned-out, compassionate heart. It is the open heart that allows you to be truly present to another human being's intimate pain.

As a bereavement caregiver, I am a companion, not a "guide"—which assumes a knowledge of another's soul I cannot claim. To companion our fellow humans means to watch and learn. Our awareness of the need to learn (as opposed to our tendency to play the expert) is the essence of true companioning.

A central role of the companion to a mourner is related to the art of honoring stories. Honoring stories requires that we slow down, turn inward and really listen as people acknowledge the reality of loss, embrace pain, review memories, and search for meaning.

The philosophy and practice of companioning interfaces naturally with hospitality. Hospitality is the essence of knowing how to live in society. Among the ancient Greeks, hospitality was a necessary element of day-to-day life. In a land where borders were permeable, it was important to get to know one's neighbors as potential friends. One way to do this was to share meals together. First, the guest and host would pour a libation to the gods. Then they would eat ("break bread") together. Then, after the guest was full, they would tell each other their stories with the guest going first. Often, tears were shed as their stories were highly personal; battles, family, histories and life tragedies all were a part of these stories. After the evening together, the host and guest were potential allies. Still today, oftentimes "breaking bread together" and then "telling personal stories" are key elements of companioning people in grief.

Henri Nouwen once elegantly described hospitality as the "creation of a free space where the stranger can enter and become a friend instead of an enemy." He observed that hospitality is not about trying to change people, but offering them space where change can take place.

He astutely noted that "hospitality is not a subtle invitation to adopt the lifestyle of the host, but the gift of a chance for the guest to find his own."

Also interesting to note is that the *Oxford English Dictionary* defines "companion" as "to accompany, to associate, to comfort, to be familiar with." This definition is actually illustrative of what it means to companion. In one sense, the notion is of comforting someone, which relates clearly to what a mourner needs and deserves. In another sense, the notion is of knowing someone, being familiar with that person's experiences and needs; this notion clearly relates to the process of becoming familiar (being open to being taught by another), which can take place through the "telling of the story."

In sum, companioning is the art of bringing comfort to another by becoming familiar with her story (experiences and needs). To companion the grieving person, therefore, is to break bread literally or figuratively, as well as listen to the story of the other. Of course this may well involve tears and sorrow and tends to involve a give and take of story: I tell you my story and you tell me yours. It is a sharing in a deep and profound way.

The sad reality is that being a fellow companion in contemporary times seems to be a lost art. Many people (including trained mental health caregivers) may not know how to truly listen, really hear, and realize how to honor another person's story. I often say, "It's not so much what is new in grief care, it is what we lost that we once had."

Advocating for the "Companioning" Model of Grief Care

A not-so-secret hope of mine is that the philosophical model of companioning explored in this book will eventually replace the more traditional medical model, which teaches that grief's goal is movement from illness to normalcy. The companioning philosophy empathizes with the human need to mourn authentically without any sense of shame. The companioning model encourages every one of us to discover how loss has forever changed us. The companioning model understands the normalcy of drowning in your grief before you tread

Treatment vs. Companioning
For Spiritual, Emotional, Existential Issues

Treatment Model	Companioning Model
To return the mourner to a prior state of homeostatic balance ("old normal").	Emphasizes the transformative, life-changing experience of grief ("new normal").
Control or stop distressful symptoms; distress is bad.	Observe, "watch out for" "bear witness" and see value in soul-based symptoms of grief
Follows a prescriptive model where counselor is perceived as expert.	Bereaved person guides the journey; "teach me" is the foundational principle.
Pathology rooted in sustained relationship to dead person.	Is a normal shift from relationship of presence to relationship of memory.
Positions the griever in a passive role.	Recognizes the need for mourner to actively mourn.
Grieving person ranges from compliant to noncompliant.	Grieving person expresses the reality of being "torn apart" as best he can.
Quality of care judged by how well grief was "managed."	Quality of care monitored by how well we allowed the griever to lead the journey.
Denial interferes with efficient integration of the loss and must be overcome.	Denial helps sustain the integration of the loss from head to heart. It is matched with patience and compassion.
Establish control; create strategic plan of intervention.	Show up with curiosity; willingness to learn from the griever.
Provide satisfactory answers for all emotional, spiritual questions and dilemmas.	Honor the mystery; facilitate the continuing "search for meaning"; no urgency to solve or satisfy the dilemma.

water, and that only after treading water do you go on to swim. The companioning model helps the caregiver acknowledge the responsibility for creating conditions that allow the grieving person to embrace the wilderness of grief.

My Principles of "Companioning" the Bereaved

Outlined below are twenty principles that undergird my work with bereaved persons and families. My hope is that you will challenge yourself to write out whatever supports you in your own work with the bereaved.

For the Companion Counselor…

1. …bereavement, grief and mourning are normal experiences; however, they are often traumatic and transformative.

2. …the helping process is seen as a collaborative, companioning process between people. The traditional medical model of mental health care is seen as inadequate and as a complicater to mobilizing the resources of the bereaved person. As a companion, I try to create conditions that engage people actively in the reconciliation needs of mourning.

3. …true expertise in grief lies with (and only with) the unique person who is grieving. Only he can be the expert of his grief. The companion is there to learn from the griever and to bear witness to and normalize his grief journey.

4. …the foundation upon which helping the bereaved person takes place is in the context of an encouraging, hope-filled relationship between the counselor and the bereaved person. The widely acknowledged core conditions of helping (empathy, warmth and caring, genuineness, respect) are seen as essential ingredients in working with bereaved people and families.

5. …traditional mental health diagnostic categories are seen as limitations on the helping process. The concept of "gardening" as opposed to "assessing" better describes efforts to understand the meaning of the death in the bereaved person's life. I strive to understand not only the bereaved person's potential complications of the grief journey, but also individual strengths and levels of wellness.

6...the counseling model is holistic in nature and views bereaved people as physical, emotional, cognitive, social and spiritual beings. Each person is unique, and seeks not just to "be," but to become.

7...the undergirding theoretical model is systems-oriented and sees the bereaved person as being impacted by interdependent relationships with persons, groups, institutions and society.

8...the focus of companioning the bereaved person is balanced between the past, the present and the future. Learning about past life experiences (particularly family of origin influences), and the nature of the relationship between the bereaved person and the person who died helps me understand the meaning of the death and the grief and mourning process for this unique person.

9...a bereaved person's perception of her reality is her reality. A "here and now" understanding of that reality allows me to be with her where she is instead of trying to push her somewhere she is not. I will be a more effective helper if I remember to enter into a person's feelings without having a need to change her feelings.

10...a major helping goal is to provide a "safe place" for the bereaved person to do the "work of mourning," resulting in healing and growth. A bereaved person does not have an illness I need to cure. I'm a caregiver, not a cure-giver!

11...people are viewed from a multicultural perspective. What is considered "normal" in one culture may be perceived as "abnormal" in another culture. On a shrinking planet, my caring and concern must be global in its perspective.

12...spiritual and religious concerns and needs are seen as central to the reconciliation process. To be an effective counselor, I must be tuned into helping people grow in depth and vitality in their spiritual and religious lives as they search for meaning and purpose in their continued living.

13...men and woman are seen in androgynous ways that encourage understanding beyond traditional sex role stereotypes. Artful companions understand that bonded relationships can exist beyond the bounds of traditional male-female partnerships acknowledged only by marriage.

14...the overall goal of helping the bereaved is reconciliation, not resolution. As companion, I have a responsibility to help the bereaved person not return to an "old normal," but to discover how the death changes her in many different ways. Traditional mental health models that teach resolution as the helping goal are seen as self-limiting and potentially destructive to the bereaved person.

15...right-brain methods of healing and growth (intuitive, metaphoric) are seen as valuable and are integrated with left-brain methods (intentional, problem solving approaches). This synergy encourages a more growth-filled approach to bereavement caregiving than do historical mental health models (primarily based on left-brain methods) of caregiving.

16..."complicated" mourning is perceived as blocked growth. The "complicated mourner" probably simply needs help in understanding the central needs of mourning and how to embrace them in ways that help him heal. Most people are where they are in their grief journeys for one of two major reasons: 1) That is where they need to be at this point in their journey; or, 2) They need, yet lack, an understanding, safe place for mourning and a person who can help facilitate their work of mourning in more growth-producing, hope-filled ways.

17...helping avenues must be adapted to the unique needs of the bereaved person. Some people are responsive to group work, some to individual work, and some to family systems work. Many people are best served, in fact, by seeking support from lay companions who have walked before them in the grief journey.

18...there is a commitment to using educational, primary prevention efforts to impact societal change because we live in a "mourning-avoidant" culture. I have a responsibility to inform other people throughout the world of the need to create safe places for people to mourn in healthy ways.

19...there is a responsibility to create conditions for healing to take place in the bereaved person. The ultimate responsibility for eventual healing lies within the person. I must remember to be responsible *to* bereaved people, not responsible *for* them.

20...excellent self-care is essential, for it provides the physical, spiritual, emotional, social and cognitive renewal necessary for the counselor to be an effective, ongoing companion in grief.

Exploring the Purpose of This Resource

This book is born out of a desire to help interested persons learn more about the philosophy of companioning people in grief. I have attempted to bring to this book what I have discovered are essential ways of being for caregivers who wish to help people experiencing grief. Obviously, this book subscribes to a relational model of caregiving rather than a medical model of caregiving. This book acknowledges a personal reality of loss for each different person. This book acknowledges the uniqueness of the response to the loss of the same person, even for people living in the same family environment. This book recognizes that people must be active participants in mourning, not passive recipients of treatment from so-called grief experts. This book is anchored in a transformative, life-changing understanding of grief.

This is NOT a book about tools and techniques. You will not find in-depth theoretical discussions based on empirical studies. While I do not intend to minimize the contributions of outcome studies and evaluations of specific techniques and approaches to bereavement counseling, they are not what I wanted to bring to this book. If that is what you are seeking, you won't have to look very far!

Also, I want to acknowledge the reality that some mourners need more counseling support than the companioning model offers. In my experience, a small percentage—fewer than ten percent—of grievers suffer from what I call "complicated mourning." Their grief journeys have been naturally complicated by multiple losses, disenfranchised grief, prior emotional struggles or other challenges. If you are companioning someone whose mourning seems complicated by other issues and you find yourself feeling at a loss, consider referring the mourner to someone who has the background and experience to provide the necessary help.

My hope is that you have already discovered that this book is different than most books you have read about grief counseling. Be assured this is a book focused more on a helping attitude or philosophy than it is a resource on what "to do." If this sounds interesting to you, please read on! If it doesn't, you may find other books more suited to your needs.

I believe that supporting people in grief is more of an art than a science. An artist fully embraces his or her personal strengths and limitations to evolve a unique style that becomes a portrait of oneself as a counselor and as a human being. I think it is a privilege to share my canvas with you and I invite you to develop your own personal counselor-as-artist way of being! Obviously, counseling models for supporting people in grief can be viewed as portraits of the people who paint them. No two portraits are or should be exactly alike. As I uncover my portrait and share it with you, my hope is you will continue painting your own unique picture of what helps you become a "safe person" for people in grief.

The book's organization is very easy to follow: The Introduction provides the backdrop and rationale for the book. Part One explores the tenets of companioning and Part Two takes you from the philosophy to practical application.

An Invitation to "Read Between the Lines"

I once heard someone say, "The truth comes in the silence between the words. It is grasped and experienced with the heart." My hope is that you, as the reader of this book, will attempt to do just that—to listen with your heart to the silence between the words. Listen to your heart and reflect on what the tenets of companioning the bereaved bring up for you. Use this opportunity to explore your own personal relationship with grief and loss.

When I was a teenager I had a dream of having a healing center where bereavement caregivers could come together and explore how we could be empowered to be agents of wholeness in the lives of the bereaved. I have taken that dream, clung to it, nurtured it and never let it go. That dream, shaped by losses in my youth, ultimately transformed my life and brought me tremendous meaning and joy in my life.

I truly believe we are all here to, in part, contribute love and care to those our lives touch—each of us in his own way. Supporting my fellow human beings in grief nourishes my soul. If you are attempting to support people in grief from a place of open-heartedness and love, you are indeed nourishing your own soul and the souls of those you touch.

A very wise person once said, "I just try to tell my own truth and sing my own song coherently, hoping that good things will come out if it. I hope others will join in singing their own song, too." This book is one attempt to sing my song. Thanks for listening and I wish you well in singing yours.

Sincerely,

Alan D. Wolfelt

The Tenets of Companioning the Bereaved

Tenet One

Companioning is about being present to another person's pain; it is not about taking away the pain.

Tenet Two

Companioning is about going to the wilderness of the soul with another human being; it is not about thinking you are responsible for finding the way out.

Tenet Three

Companioning is about honoring the spirit; it is not about focusing on the intellect.

Tenet Four

Companioning is about listening with the heart; it is not about analyzing with the head.

Tenet Five

Companioning is about bearing witness to the struggles of others; it is not about judging or directing these struggles.

Tenet Six

Companioning is about walking alongside; it is not about leading or being led.

Tenet Seven

Companioning means discovering the gifts of sacred silence; it does not mean filling up every moment with words.

Tenet Eight

Companioning is about being still; it is not about frantic movement forward.

Tenet Nine

Companioning is about respecting disorder and confusion; it is not about imposing order and logic.

Tenet Ten

Companioning is about learning from others; it is not about teaching them.

Tenet Eleven

Companioning is about curiosity; it is not about expertise.

"In every heart there is an inner room, where we can hold our greatest treasures and our deepest pain."—Marianne Williamson

---

Tenet One

Companioning is about being present to another person's pain; it is not about taking away the pain.

To be bereaved literally means to be "torn apart." When someone is torn apart, there is a natural need to embrace the heartfelt pain of the loss. There is no pill we can take to relieve the pain and suffering, and no surgery that can reassemble the pieces of a broken heart. The way in which we care for fellow humans who are suffering the pain of loss has much to do with the ways in which we will be able to supportively companion others.

"The word care implies a way of responding to expressions of the soul that is not heroic and muscular."
—Thomas Moore

Sadly, current North American culture often makes the person in grief feel intense shame and embarrassment about feelings of pain and suffering. People who are perceived as "doing well" with their grief are considered "strong" and "under control." Society erroneously implies that if grieving people openly express feelings of pain and suffering, they are immature or overly emotional.

In contemporary North American culture, pain and feelings of loss are experiences most people try to avoid. Why? Because the role of suffering is misunderstood. Normal thoughts and feelings that result from loss are typically seen as unnecessary and inappropriate. Yet, only in gathering courage to move toward this hurt is anyone able to ultimately heal.

Grief Is Not Shameful

As the bereaved experience grief, they are often greeted with what I call "buck-up therapy"—messages like "carry on," "keep your chin up," or "just keep busy." And combined with these messages is often another unstated but strong belief: "You have a right not to hurt—so do whatever is necessary to avoid it." In sum, the person in grief is often encouraged to deny, avoid, or numb themselves to the pain of the experience.

When personal feelings of grief are met with shame-based messages or silent indifference, discovering how to integrate the loss becomes all but impossible. If the bereaved person internalizes stated and unstated messages that encourage the repression, avoidance, or numbing of grief, they often become powerless to help themselves. I often say that finding the way into and through grief is often more difficult than finding a way beyond it. In fact, internalizing the belief that mourning is wrong or bad tempts many people to act as if they feel better than they really do. Ultimately, denying the grief denies one the essence of life and puts one at risk for living in the "shadow of the ghosts of grief."

❖❖❖❖❖❖❖❖❖❖❖❖❖

"Man could not live if he were entirely impervious to sadness. Many sorrows can be endured only by being embraced… Melancholy is morbid only when it occupies too much place in life; but it is equally morbid for it to be wholly excluded from life." —Emile Durkheim

❖❖❖❖❖❖❖❖❖❖❖❖❖

When we as caregivers experience the pain and suffering of a fellow human being, we instinctively want to take the pain away. Yet, to truly companion another human being requires that we sit with the pain as we overcome the instinct to want to "fix." We may discover that we want to fix another's pain because it is hurting us too much.

Suffering doesn't mean something is wrong. It isn't happening because we made the wrong move or said the wrong thing. As Thomas Moore wisely noted, "The basic intention of any caring—physical or psycho-

Courage

The word courage comes from the French word for heart (coeur). Courage grows for those things in life that impact us deeply. The death of someone treasured opens, or engages, our hearts. Then we must take our hearts, which have been engaged, and muster the courage to encounter any and all feelings, including pain and suffering. Courage can also be defined as the ability to do what one believes is right, despite the fact that others may strongly and persuasively disagree.

❖❖❖❖❖❖❖❖❖❖❖❖❖❖❖❖❖❖❖❖❖❖❖❖❖❖❖❖❖❖❖❖❖❖❖

❖❖❖❖❖❖❖❖❖❖❖❖❖❖❖❖❖❖❖❖❖❖❖❖❖❖❖❖❖❖❖❖❖❖❖

The Shadow of the Ghosts of Grief

The person who is living in the shadow of the ghosts of grief has symptoms that suggest that the pain of grief has been inhibited, suppressed or denied. These symptoms are staying present, driving the person's life, trying to get the attention they deserve.

Potential symptoms include, but are not limited to,:
- negative outlook on life
- generalized anxiety
- addictive behaviors
- low-grade depression
- difficulty in intimate relationships
- unconscious despair
- chronic anhedonia (the inability to find pleasure in normally pleasurable activities)

To suppress the pain of grief is to condemn oneself to a living death. Living fully means feeling fully; it means being completely one with what you are experiencing. If a person is unwilling or unable to integrate loss into her life, she will project her symptoms into her body, her relationships and her worldview. The old, unhealed wounds of grief will linger, influencing all aspects of her life, her living, and, particularly, her loving.

❖❖❖❖❖❖❖❖❖❖❖❖❖❖❖❖❖❖❖❖❖❖❖❖❖❖❖❖❖❖❖❖❖❖❖

logical—is to alleviate suffering. But in relation to the symptom itself, observance means first of all listening and looking carefully at what is being revealed in the suffering. An intent to heal can get in the way of seeing. By doing less, more is accomplished."

> "It is possible, in fact, to validate someone's feelings while at the same time validating their capacity to move beyond those feelings."
>
> —Marianne Williamson

Ultimately, if we rush in to take away a person's grief pain, we also take away the opportunity for her to integrate the loss into her life. To be truly a healing presence, we must be able to share another person's pain while realizing there is nothing we can do to instantly relieve it and knowing that we are not responsible for it— all the while seeking to empathetically understand what the pain feels like. The paradox of entering into the pain lies in the truth that as you affirm someone's feelings of suffering, you are also affirming his eventual capacity to move beyond those feelings. As Helen Keller taught us years ago, "The only way to the other side is through."

The Wisdom of the Soul

Yes, sometimes it may seem as if you are "doing" very little as you open your heart to a fellow struggler. And yet this is an example of how companioning inspires an attribute of the soul: wisdom. Wisdom is the sense of recognizing that in your helplessness you ultimately become helpful. A wise caregiver will have the wisdom to know what she can do, accept what she can't do, and have the spirit of the heart engaged in ways that can and do make a difference.

In providing a soulful response to another person's pain, we must discover and nurture two qualities that are within us: humility and "unknowing." We must first be present with an open mind and an open heart. To be open in this way of being is not an absence of thought, however. In fact, it is a clear, focused attentiveness to the moment. It is about immediacy—being present in the here and now.

When we as caregivers focus the power of our attention on the suffering of another human being, the full measure of our soul becomes available to her. Releasing any preconceptions of the need to take away pain allows our hearts to open wide and be infinitely more present, loving and compassionate. Presence in the fullness of the moment is where the soul resides.

And being present to people in the pain of their grief is about being present to them in their "soul work." There is a lovely Jungian distinction between "soul work" and "spirit work."

Soul work: a downward movement in the psyche; a willingness to connect with what is dark, deep, and not necessarily pleasant.

Spirit work: a quality of moving toward the light; upward, ascending.

In part, being present to another person's pain of grief is about being willing to descend with them into their soul work—which precedes their spirit work. A large part of being present to someone in soul work is to bear witness to the pain and suffering and not to think of it as a door to someplace else. This can help keep you in the moment. Dark, deep and unpleasant emotions need to be held in the same way happiness and joy need to be held—with respect and humility.

> "You must descend before you can transcend."
> —Alan Wolfelt

> "A wound that goes unacknowledged and unwept is a wound that cannot heal."
> —John Eldredge

Acknowledging Our Own Suffering

As our hearts begin to open to the presence of suffering, challenging thoughts may creep in. Can I really help this person? Is the pain of his loss touching my own losses? If I reach out to support, what will happen to me? In the push-pull this experience triggers, there is little wonder that being present to the suffering of others seems so difficult.

The capacity to acknowledge our own discomfort when confronted with suffering is usually less overwhelming when it is no longer minimized or denied. To give attention to our helplessness can free us to open more fully to another as well as to our own pain and suffering. We no longer find ourselves wanting to run away. We can slow down, be still and open to the presence of the pain. We can witness what is without feeling the need to fix it!

When we become conscious that any part of us wants to run away from the pain, we can gently embrace it; an entire new level of receptiveness becomes possible. As we become the companion, we begin to see what is being asked of us that is not so much about "doing" but instead about "being." We discover what anxieties and fears might be inhibiting our helping hearts, and come to trust the healing power of presence.

Finally, we can begin to listen—truly listen and give honor to the pain. Instead of pushing away suffering or merely releasing the need to "fix" it, we are able to enter into it. We are not indifferent or passive; we are fully available and open. We are truly being hospitable to the pain of another person.

Soullessness and the Divine Spark

In my experience, soul is real, authentic and vital. When a mourner says, "I'm not sure I want to go on living," she is expressing a loss of her authenticity, her vitality. She is expressing what I call "soullessness." Part of the role of the companion is to be patiently present to her in ways that stir the vital force within her and help her discover renewed connection to the greater world of humanity. Companioning is, in part, the conduit through which the mourner can search for and find what Meister Eckhart termed the "divine spark"—that which gives depth and purpose to our living. What an honor to help relight the divine spark!

In opening to our own suffering from life losses, we enhance our desire to be of service to those around us. We become truly available at deeper levels of our souls. We do not deny pain but open to it and learn what it is trying to teach us. In becoming more sensitive and responsive to one's own pain as well as the pain of others, we continue to see ourselves as students always learning to become more heartfelt companions to our fellow strugglers. What an honor!

✦✦✦✦✦✦✦✦✦✦✦✦✦✦✦✦✦✦✦✦✦

"There are in many of us wounds so deep that only the mediation of someone else to whom we can bare our grief can heal us." —Agnes Sanford

✦✦✦✦✦✦✦✦✦✦✦✦✦✦✦✦✦✦✦✦✦

"The only map that does the spiritual traveler any good is the one that leads to the center."—Christina Baldwin

Tenet Two

Companioning is about going to the wilderness of the soul with another human being; it is not about thinking you are responsible for finding the way out.

When someone we love dies and we feel suffering, it does not mean that something is wrong. Going into the wilderness of the soul with another human being is anchored in walking with them through spiritual distress without thinking we have to have them attain "resolution" or "recovery."

Being in the wilderness relates to being in a liminal space. "Limina" is the Latin word for threshold, the space betwixt and between. Liminal space is that spiritual place where most people hate to be, but where the experience of grief leads them. This is often where the griever's worldview—the set of beliefs about how the world functions and what place they as individuals occupy therein—comes into question. Putting one's shattered worldview back together paradoxically requires companions who do not think their helping role is to fix or give answers or explanations. There is no technique, no formula, no prescription for the wilderness experience.

A critical part of being present to someone in the wilderness of the soul is to be open to states of not knowing the outcome or trying to force the outcome. Most North Americans have trouble trusting in this process and feel an instinctive need to get the mourner out of the wilderness, or, at the very least, to try to move her to the left or the right. We have become a people who demand answers, explanations and expect fast and efficient resolutions.

The Ambiguity of Loss

We don't like pain, sadness, anxiety, ambiguity, loss of control—all normal symptoms of the wilderness of grief. We want to experience light before we encounter darkness. If we as caregivers cannot be still in the presence of these care-eliciting symptoms, we will be tempted to explain or treat them away. After all, we falsely think that any explanation is better than being in liminal space. A sense of control is better than the terrible "cloud of unknowing." Yet, the opposite of control is actually participation—in this context, participation in the work of mourning while one is "under reconstruction."

The challenge for many caregivers is to stay on the threshold of the wilderness without consciously or unconsciously demanding or projecting a desire for resolution. In other words, there is a tendency to be attached to outcome, not open to outcome. Obviously, the instinct to move the mourner away from pain and suffering is rooted in the desire to stay distant from one's own pain.

Sadly, many people, caregivers and lay public alike, have come to regard grief as an enemy. Brokenness is not something we choose to invite in. Instead of honoring the wise words of Joseph Addison, who once said "I will indulge my sorrows, and give way to all the pangs and fury of despair," our contemporary mantra seems to be more aligned with the words of the Bobby McFerrin song: "Don't Worry, Be Happy!"

❖❖❖❖❖❖❖❖❖❖❖❖❖❖❖❖❖❖❖❖❖❖❖❖❖❖❖❖❖❖

Under Reconstruction

To be bereaved literally means "to be torn apart." When someone has been torn apart by grief, they are in essence "under reconstruction." Maslow's famous hierarchy of human needs teaches us that our most fundamental needs—for shelter, food, water, sleep—must first be met before we can meet our higher order needs. Thus the mourner's physical needs must be taken care of, followed, in Maslow's order, by his needs for safety, love/belonging, esteem and actualization. To heal, he must reconstruct his entire life from the ground up.

❖❖❖❖❖❖❖❖❖❖❖❖❖❖❖❖❖❖❖❖❖❖❖❖❖❖❖❖❖❖

The No Place That Is Grief

In contrast, ancient cultures seemed to understand the value of being in the wilderness as a part of any kind of major transition in life's journey. They often invited themselves into the wilderness through experiences such as spending 40 days in the desert, climbing to the mountaintops, and taking solo journeys into the ocean. Whatever the underlying set of beliefs, to get where he was eventually going the journeyer first had to experience going to nowhere, to release himself from who and what he had been.

In the "no place" of the wilderness he could begin building a new person and place again.

"The clearest way into the universe is through a forest wilderness."—John Muir

This resonates with my experience of companioning people in life transitions. It seems we cannot integrate loss into our lives until we embrace the fear and sometimes raw terror of going to this "no place" wilderness and descending into it on our way through it. Then and only then do we begin to notice that something begins to slowly shift as we open our hearts to the pain of grief.

Of course, there are powerful forces that invite mourners to do otherwise. We are told to "keep busy," "carry on" and "find someone to meet." Following these mourning-avoidant scripts, the griever may try to retrace her steps back to a time or place that feels familiar, a place to find one's "old self"—but that old self is gone forever. Now, being temporarily lost in the wilderness of grief is that familiar place. Slowly, over time and with gentle companions, the mourner can search for renewed meaning and discover a new self.

But through this time of turmoil, the discomfort and mystery of being in the wilderness is meant to be. In reality, it is actually a kind of "purification phase"—it is just one phase of the journey that will very slowly change into something else. The important thing is to learn to honor and respect this process and to lean into it despite the instinct to do otherwise.

No, it is not comfortable to be betwixt and between—to be helpless, out of control, depressed, anxious, and to not know. Again, if we look to other cultures we discover that in parts of Africa, a person who is in a place of not knowing is considered to be in a place of "walking the land of gray clouds." During times of uncertainty and not knowing, it is considered inappropriate, even foolish, to take action. In fact, it is considered an act of wisdom to wait and trust the process. The opposite of trusting the process is trying to control the uncontrollable—obviously an impossible task when it involves experiences of grief and mourning.

Detachment and Grief

Central to not being attached to outcome is the concept of detachment. The majority of Westerners think of "detachment" as a lack of warmth and caring. Yet, linguistically, the word detachment is often defined as "the capacity to come deeply from an objective place." Considered from this perspective, detachment can be

"Our work in psychology would change remarkably if we thought about it as ongoing care rather than as a quest for the cure... Care of the soul observes the paradox whereby a muscled, strong-willed pursuit of change can actually stand in the way of substantive transformation."
—Thomas Moore

Divine Momentum

In grief, Divine Momentum is the notion that the process of mourning will, all by itself, lead to healing and reconciliation. In embracing and expressing their grief, mourners will, over time and with the support of others, move forward. To trust in Divine Momentum is to believe that healing can and will unfold. As companion, you help create Divine Momentum for healing by offering a safe starting place for the journey. You offer a free and open space for mourners to give attention to that which they need to give attention to.

seen as not trying to control what you can't control. In part, it is "going with the symptom." It is observing what the soul is teaching about the depth of feeling and not trying to change it. You stay present to what is without thinking you need to change it or take it away. You observe the soul; you don't mask or try to do away with symptoms of soul work. All this time, you stay patient and recognize that going through grief is more necessary than going around it or moving beyond it.

When you are detached, you are still very much present to the deep soul work that is taking place. This is about not getting pulled in to feeling responsible for taking away the pain of the loss. Actually, you care deeply in a way that allows you to be totally present to what is there rather than what you wish was there. You could consider this a homeopathic response of going with what is presented as opposed to against it. You are open to outcome, not attached to outcome! Or, as the Zen statement observes in a lovely way, "Spring comes, and the grass grows all by itself." The companion is able to acknowledge that less effort is sometimes better.

New Models of Grief Care

This orientation to caring is in contrast to modern psychological approaches that tend toward a more rational and logical understanding of matters of the heart. Modern psychology invites people to identify a problem and fix it. "Managed care" is just that—managed care. Very few models exist wherein we see the value of soul and symptoms of distress that need to be reflected on, observed, and respected.

We need soul-based models of caring that demonstrate the sensitivity of the heart. We need models that allow mourners to stay open to the mystery as they encounter the wilderness of their grief. We need models that respect that we don't have to understand and control everything that surrounds us. In fact, perhaps it is in "standing under" the mysterious experience of death that provides us with a unique perspective. We are not above or bigger than death. Maybe only after discovering the liminal space of the wilderness, in which we do not "understand," can we patiently discover renewed meaning and purpose in our continued living.

Surrendering To Grief

In my experience, "understanding" comes when we as companions help the grievers surrender: surrender any need to compare their grief (it's not a competition); surrender any self-critical judgments (self-compassion is a critical ingredient to integrating loss into life); and surrender any need to completely understand (we never do because mystery is something to be pondered, not explained).

"There sometimes seems to be an inverse relationship between information and wisdom... We have many demanding academic programs in professional psychology, and states often have rigid requirements for the practice of psychotherapy, and yet there is undoubtedly a severe dearth of wisdom about the mysteries of the soul."
—Thomas Moore

The grief that touches our souls has its own voice and should not be compromised by a need for comparison, judgment, or even complete understanding. Actually, surrendering to the unknowable wilderness of grief is a courageous choice, an act of faith, a trust in God and in oneself. The grieving person can only hold this mystery in her heart and surround herself with compassionate, non-judgmental companions. My hope is that is YOU—the reader of this book.

For transformation of grief to unfold, you have to surrender to the experience. Trying to stay in control by denying, inhibiting or converting grief can result in what Kierkegaard termed "unconscious despair." Doing the soul work of grief demands going into and through suffering and integrating it in ways that help unite you with your fellow strugglers and the greater community of people.

John Keats observed in Shakespeare what he called a "negative capability"…"the capacity to be in mystery and doubt without any irritable searching after fact and reason." I have discovered that one way to survive the wilderness experience is to remember that you are doing the hard work of mourning even when you may seem to be doing nothing. And even when the mourner feels like he is making the slowest of progress and edging out of the deep wilderness, there will be times when he will feel like he is backtracking and being ravaged by the forces around him. This, too, is the nature of grief. Complete mastery of a wilderness experience is not possible. Just as we cannot control the winds and storms and the beasts in nature, we can never have total dominion over our grief. However, as the griever experiences the wilderness, he both needs and deserves caring companions along the way.

"The ultimate cure, as many ancient and modern psychologies of depth have asserted, comes from love and not from logic."—Thomas Moore

---

Tenet Three

Companioning is about honoring the spirit; it is not about focusing on the intellect.

To be torn apart and to then become whole again we need more than our intellect. We need the experiences that spring from the spirit and the soul. "Spirit" can be broadly defined as our nonphysical essences, which include dimensions of intellect, emotion, personality and spirituality. I often perceive the spirit as the "life-force." As human beings we are spirit explorers who have stepped into bodies here on earth.

"Soul" is not a thing but a quality or dimension of experiencing life. Thomas Moore notes that soul "has to do with depth, value, relatedness, heart and personal substance." If you wish to companion people in grief, I believe you must be present to matters of the spirit and soul.

Obviously, we as humans seek protection from raw emotions by, at times, intellectualizing the experiences of grief. We move back and forth between head and heart, between intellect and feeling. I submit that in contemporary North America we are often invited to think around losses instead of feel them through. We bring to grief a fix-it attitude, assuming that the experience is something to be overcome and that you would be well served to "let go" of it and move on quickly and efficiently.

Yet, matters of the spirit and soul are not dedicated to letting go and moving on in some perfectionist, intellectual fashion. If we want to give attention to the spirit and the soul, then we have to discard the "resolution wish" and give care in ways that respect the energy of grief. As John Donne, the poet of relationship and soul once observed, "He who has no time to mourn, has no time to mend." Respect for grief demands our appreciation for its complexity.

Accepting What Is

When we look at the spirit and soul of grief, we discover value in slowing down and not trying to take away painful emotions that are a necessary part of the journey. If we join the griever in only trying to think through loss, we are trying to avoid the reaches of the spirit and the soul. When you as a caregiver give attention to the messages from the spirit and soul, you empathize with the uncomfortable thoughts and feelings that are inherent to the journey.

Working within this premise encourages you to support the grieving person in taking back what she is often trying to intellectually disown, such as depression, anxiety and loss of control. As opposed to wishing they weren't there, you work with the raw emotions by entering into them. Instead of trying to manage the grief the person is experiencing, you realize the value of the grief managing the person. As the Greek philosopher Heraclitus observed many years ago, "The soul has its own source of unfolding."

A homeopathic response to grief is to go with what is presented rather than against it. We befriend grief instead of making an enemy of it. Instead of trying to quickly get away from our grief, we savor it.

❖❖❖❖❖❖❖❖❖❖❖❖❖❖

"All suffering prepares the soul for vision."—Martin Buber

❖❖❖❖❖❖❖❖❖❖❖❖❖❖

If the griever is experiencing deep sadness, then the spirit and soul are expressing the rhythms of the journey into and through grief. Instead of trying to outmaneuver these forces and use some premature technique to return life to "normal" (an inappropriate helping goal), I submit that the more authentic way of being in tune with the soul is in the direction of the symptoms. Any other response is like fighting with what the spirit and soul are bringing forth.

Have you noticed how depression has gotten a bad name these days? It's like we expect we have some God-given right to never be depressed. Yet, in my experience, normal life circumstances, such as the death of someone precious to us, can naturally result in depression, particularly if defined in the following way:

Depression: A turning inward when the world outside no longer seems to be charged with meaning and purpose.

Respecting the Work of the Soul

I find that as a companion who tries to be respectful of soul and spirit work, my role is to empathize with what is being expressed in the moment. For example, if a person comes into my Center for Loss and says, "I can't get my feet out of bed in the morning," my responsibility is not to use some technique to help this person overcome the lethargy of grief accompanied by profound sadness. Instead, my role is to empathize with what it is like to be a lost spirit and soul. I try to help the mourner embrace her soul work: "Someone precious has died. I feel so alone right now. My body, spirit and soul are depressed. I lack meaning and purpose in my daily life right now. What am I trying to experience so that slowly, over time, I can discover renewed meaning in my life?" This is the kind of empathetic responsiveness that helps create a non-judgmental companioning relationship with this person.

Being respectful might lead me to simply respond in ways that encourage her to be self-compassionate about the normalcy of the physical and emotional symptoms of her grief. I might restate for her, "So, right now, it's hard to get your feet out of bed." My response to people in grief is based on the belief that the only way beyond the experience of grief is through the experience of grief. The mourner must descend before she can transcend. Many contemporary "therapies" get this descend–transcend experience out of order.

Yes, when the spirit and soul of grief come to life in grief, the ordinary wisdom or intellectual life loses much of its power. To avoid our own pain, we may be tempted to offer up some rational advice like, "Being depressed isn't going to bring the person who died back." Yet, these kind of rationalizations are not helpful in the end. Repression of the voices of the spirit and soul only serve to move the griever further away from the ultimate integration of the death into her life. Even depression has the capacity to propel the mourner to insights that can result in eventual renewal.

◇◇◇◇◇◇◇◇◇◇◇◇◇

"Do you not see how necessary a world of pains and troubles is to school an intelligence and make it a soul?"—John Keats

"I never came upon any of my discoveries through the process of rational thinking."
—Albert Einstein

◇◇◇◇◇◇◇◇◇◇◇◇◇

Honoring the spirit and soul is about being honest about the sting of grief and acknowledging the reality of the depth of the loss. Some native cultures describe "speaking with spirit tongue" when they emphasize the importance of being honest and telling the truth. Honoring the spirit and soul is what I refer to as "listening with the spirit ear," wherein you witness the honest pain of the loss and affirm the need of the mourner to tell the truth about the transformational journey of grief.

In reflecting on the vital importance of honoring the spirit and soul of grief, I think about the shamanic concept of sacred hoops, which is synonymous with the term "authenticity" or being connected to your own spirituality. The idea is that when you experience being yourself, you are in your sacred hoop, and when you are being genuinely who you are without pretense, you are sitting inside your sacred hoop. Being truly who you are when companioning people in grief allows you to honor the spirit—the life force—of another human being.

A soul- and spirit-centered understanding of grief mandates a different language from that of traditional mental health care. We companion our fellow strugglers by honoring their expressions of grief, recognizing that spirit and soul have their own purposes, and supporting them more from our hearts than from our heads.

Tenet Four

Companioning is about listening with the heart; it is not about analyzing with the head

Scientific analyses about grief and therapeutic theories surrounding interventions often result in caregivers overlooking the sacred art of listening with the heart. In fact, there are a multitude of invitations to use your head to assess, diagnose, and treat, which, by default, encourage you to stay distant from the heart.

Our language is replete with references to the heart that give testimony to our instinctual understanding of this part of our divinity and humanity: "Take heart;" "the heart of the matter;" and "home is where the heart is" are but a few of a multitude of references to the heart in our everyday conversations. We know deeply that authentic mourning is a quest for the healing of our broken hearts.

The heart holds answers the brain refuses to see.
—Robert Kall

My years of learning from my own losses—as well as the losses of those who have trusted me to walk with them—have taught me that the path of the heart applies to both the mourner and the companion. Listening with the heart is anchored in the capacity to express compassion and understanding and to possess a deep desire to show solidarity with people experiencing grief. Nowhere are we hungrier for more heart-based, soul-centered models than in the area of grief care.

The Power of Open-Heartedness

The good news is that as companions we can do just that—minister to people in grief from a place of open-heartedness. However, you will have to remember to be a responsible rebel—to question assumptions, to work from this attitude. Why? Because like me, probably no one in your schooling told you, "Listen with your heart. Minister to others from a place of open-heartedness." So, as I did, you may have to learn this on your own or seek out other responsible rebels as mentors.

❖❖❖❖❖❖❖❖❖❖❖❖❖❖

"Listening is an attitude of the heart, a genuine desire to be with another which both attracts and heals."
—J. Isham

❖❖❖❖❖❖❖❖❖❖❖❖❖❖

I do believe we can set our intention toward being open-hearted and then make the time and effort to bring it about. First comes the internal decision: I will work from a place of open-heartedness. There are so many forces working against this today (e.g., managed care, brief therapies, evidence-based practices, a fast-paced culture, a lack of understanding of the role of hurt in healing) that it will not happen without that internal decision. In addition, the internal decision will likely have to be based on something that has genuine meaning to you: feeling nudged that this is the way to be present to your fellow human beings; being inspired by hearing someone talk about this way of being; or an innate desire that has always been a part of who you are.

In our search for ministry from a place of open-heartedness, I reflect on the importance of four critical ingredients: humility; unknowing; unconditional love; and what I have come to call a spiritual practice of "readiness to receive" a fellow human being. Allow me to explore each one of these with you.

Humility

Humility is grounded in realizing you are not an expert about grief. You are the student who is being taught by the true expert—the person in grief. Humility is also about a willingness to learn from your mistakes as well as an appreciation of your limitations and strengths. When you come from a place of humility, your behavior is welcoming, tolerant, and nonjudgmental. You come from a place of the open soul that is totally present, compassionate, and peace-filled.

❖❖❖❖❖❖❖❖❖❖❖❖❖

"Wear your learning like your watch, in a private pocket; and do not pull it out, and strike it, merely to show that you have one."
—Lord Chesterfield

❖❖❖❖❖❖❖❖❖❖❖❖❖

Unknowing

Unknowing means being completely present to the mourner with an open mind and an open heart. This does mot mean an absence of thought, but, in contrast, a very clear attentiveness to the moment. Unknowing is not achieved by some conscious effort or technique but by letting go—giving up any need to be in control or manage someone's grief journey. Unknowing guides our hearts to the path of our soul and creates a safe space for the griever to authentically mourn. The domain of the soul is where one can encounter what is most feared and open to what it might be tempting to close oneself off from. When we initiate helping from a place of unknowing, the full measure of our soul is available to reach out in support of those in grief.

Unconditional Love and Acceptance

The very essence of open-heartedness is the capacity to express unconditional love and acceptance of the mourner. Just as love is at the center of grief, love is also the core of compassionate caregiving. Unconditional love is the expression of the Divine flowing through you with no expectations attached.

Unconditional love creates a sacred safe space for the griever to authentically mourn. At the same time, this kind of love creates a sense of personal responsibility in the mourner. As a companion, you are responsible *to* the mourner, not *for* the mourner. Part of the paradox of communicating unconditional love is that it frees the mourner to do her work instead of you thinking it is something you do for her. Unconditional love creates a safe harbor to mourn, but it does not overprotect or hinder the freedom to mourn.

❖❖❖❖❖❖❖❖❖❖❖❖❖❖❖

"Give love and unconditional acceptance to those you encounter and notice what happens."—Wayne Dyer

❖❖❖❖❖❖❖❖❖❖❖❖❖❖❖

Unconditional love elevates your caregiving to the transpersonal realm of experience. Our open hearts are able to become pathways through which Divine love is expressed to the mourner. The companion relationship becomes sacred as it basks in the wisdom and healing powers of unconditional love.

Unconditional love puts you into a "flow-like" state of being. When you are in this flow experience, you are externally focused on the moment-to-moment needs of the mourner. The mourner can actually feel and experience your heartfelt compassion. To achieve flow, you must consciously cultivate your capacity to actively express love that is revealed at the soul level.

Unconditional love is experienced and expressed on all five levels of our being: physical, cognitive, emotional, social, and spiritual. When you become committed to expressing your life energy in these five levels, you will radiate the gift and grace of unconditional love. Then you can truly be the companion you were meant to be.

Readiness to Receive

Over the years I have discovered the value of a spiritual practice I use to prepare my heart and soul to be present to mourners in ways that facilitate the expression of humility, unknowing, and unconditional love. I have come to refer to this practice as my "readiness to receive" ritual.

◇-◇

Understanding the Five Levels of Unconditional Love

Physical level: You feel a sense of lightness, a sense of warmth and caring that is felt in the throat and chest area, particularly the area of the heart; you feel relaxed and honored to be in the presence of someone willing to allow you to honor her grief journey.

Cognitive level: You are nonjudgmental and accepting of how the mourner may think differently about her grief experience than you do; you do not assess or diagnose; you "seek to understand" without judgment; you are welcoming and tolerant.

Emotional level: You feel open and present to a full spectrum of emotions, whatever they might be; you are committed to consciously exploring how your own emotions are impacted as you companion your fellow human beings; you feel emotionally congruent in your helping role and may well recognize you have found your calling.

Social level: You recognize that your capacity to create a "sacred safe space" to give attention to another's grief is at the center of the definition of mourning: "the shared social response to loss;" you are humbled that people are willing to make use of your personhood in this way; you are happy to be the companion you are; you feel your heart is at home in this helping role.

Spiritual level: You convey a sense of gentle, positive, creative energy anchored in compassion, meaning a willingness "to suffer with;" you have a desire to give to others and "walk with" or "break bread" with them; you realize you touch at the soul level when you reach out with your heart instead of your mind; you feel a trust and optimism surrounding the mourner's capacity to bring forth grief in ways that lead to healing and wholeness.

Matthew Fox, theologian and educator, wisely observed, "When we are joyous and full of heart we are emanating wisdom. Wisdom is not in the head but in the heart and gut where compassion is felt." Unconditional love is expressed through the five transpersonal levels introduced above. Once you have the courage to minister to those in grief from a place of love instead of clinical distance, you will discover your inherent passion to be a companion.

◇-◇

Just before I see anyone for support in their journey, I center myself in a quiet place, inside or outside the Center for Loss and Life Transition. By creating a sacred space and stepping away from the business of the day, I seek to find quietness and stillness. In a very real sense I'm preparing my soul to be totally present to the grieving person or family. This practice is a way of letting go of anything that might get in the way of my open-heartedness. I seem to need this time to listen to myself before I can listen to others.

Once I have gone quiet, I repeat a three-phrase mantra to myself. The three phrases are:

"No rewards for speed"

"Divine Momentum"

"Not attached to outcome"

These words help me slow down, recognize my role is to help create momentum for the griever to authentically mourn life losses, and to always remember the vital importance of being present to people where they are instead of where I might think they need to be. After repeating these phrases for two to three minutes, I usually conclude with some kind of affirmation like, "I thank the universe for providing me the opportunity to help people mourn well so they can go on to live well and love well."

Obviously, your spiritual practice of readiness to receive a fellow human being may be different than mine. Yet, I do hope you consider some ritual that propels you to a place of open-heartedness. Yes, your open heart is a well of reception; it will be moved entirely by what it perceives. Then a beautiful process unfolds: Listening and responding from the heart, you are patiently empathetic to the needs of the mourner. She then begins to sense your belief, and, more important, her own belief, in her capacity to integrate the death of someone precious into her life. You are honored and privileged to be a small part of this journey.

*"Too often we underestimate the power of a touch,
a smile, a kind word, a listening ear, an honest compliment,
or the smallest act of caring, all of which have the
potential to turn a life around."*—Leo Buscaglia

Tenet Five

Companioning is about bearing witness to the struggles of others; it is not about judging or directing these struggles.

Bearing witness to the struggles of someone experiencing the darkness of grief—having empathy—is the deepest form of emotional and spiritual interaction you can have with another human being. If you can hear another person's words of pain and loss, not from a place of clinical distance but from a place of an open heart, then you can bring a fully alive human presence to bear on the other human being's experiences. Overcoming any tendency to judge will allow you to be taught by the griever. This active empathy will naturally create an environment in which healing can and will occur.

Entering into and bearing witness to the anguish of raw grief can be overwhelming, for to actually be able to enter into another person's experience so completely that she is able to feel your companionship is the embodiment of the highest degree of emotional and spiritual refinement. To truly join the mourner in the place of her help-

$\diamond\diamond\diamond\diamond\diamond\diamond\diamond\diamond\diamond\diamond\diamond\diamond\diamond$

"Some people think only intellect counts: knowing how to solve problems, knowing how to get by, knowing how to identify an advantage and seize it. But the functions of intellect are insufficient without courage, love, friendship, compassion and empathy."
—Dean Koontz

$\diamond\diamond\diamond\diamond\diamond\diamond\diamond\diamond\diamond\diamond\diamond\diamond\diamond$

lessness requires that we as caregivers visit our own griefs and experience our transformed hearts.

Doing Your Own Work First

The supporting cradle of empathy evolves from the collage of feelings we have come to encounter in our own personal journeys into grief. You may find that if you haven't felt a particular feeling, or if you are unwilling or unable to reencounter it, your capacity to be present to another person will be inhibited. You may even see the loss as something that has happened to "her" and not to "you" and thus lose your openness, your compassionate presence. Your empathy with her struggles will be a feeble attempt at embracing the feelings, not a truly empathetic experience.

That is why bearing witness to the struggles of those in grief is such a demanding ministry. You have to do your own work first to acquaint yourself in depth with your soul-based emotions. Only then, because you have authentically felt, will you "know what it feels like." You will have an anchor in your own soul for what a grief experience may feel like to a fellow human being. Since you have been there, you can enter into struggles such as discovering a reason to go on living, redefining one's worldview, and searching for meaning in life and living.

❖❖❖❖❖❖❖❖❖❖❖❖❖

"The heart that breaks open can contain the whole universe." —Joanna Macy

"Compassion is the basis of morality." —Arnold Schopenhauer

❖❖❖❖❖❖❖❖❖❖❖❖❖

A natural inhibition in the willingness to enter into the wilderness of grief is that we are often hesitant, or literally afraid, of reopening our own wounds. Instead of being able to companion a fellow struggler, we may be overwhelmed by the conscious recreation of our own painful feelings. So, instead of being open to the presence of the pain of the loss, we may deny people their experiences ("It could be worse"): we may problem-solve or technique people ("Here's what to do so you can let go"); or we may minimize or compare experiences ("You think you have it bad? Let me tell you what happened to someone else").

To be able to enter into the wilderness with a person in the depths of grief, therefore, requires the embracing of our own heartfelt emotions, not in the sense of mastering them, but in allowing them to flow through us. Then, and only then, are we able to give the most precious gift—our compassionate companionship.

Expressing Compassion

Bearing witness to the struggles of people in grief is about having compassion. Compassion is from the words *cum pation*, meaning "to suffer with," "to undergo with," "to share solidarity with."

Compassion embraces our common humanity, our feelings of togetherness, our experiences of kinship. This word compassion has been so much in exile in the mainstream grief counseling literature, yet it is the very essence of what bereaved people both need and deserve. Therefore, the theme of this book is about healing grief as a philosophical and literal act of

"If we don't bear witness as citizens, as people, as individuals, the right that we have had to life is sacrificed. There is a silence, instead of a speaking presence."
—Jane Rule

removing the obstacles to compassion. While empathy refers to "feeling with" the grieving person, compassion is about "feeling for" the grieving person. You have to care for and about the person to be a soulful companion.

Actively expressing compassion through bearing witness to the struggles of others is by no means elitist. Anyone and everyone can express compassion to someone encountering grief. You don't have to have a college degree to express compassion. You don't have to be a certified grief counselor to express compassion. You only need to have a heart full of grace and a soul anchored in love.

Bearing Witness Means Being Involved in the Feeling World

Bearing witness to the struggle of the griever is anchored in striving to understand the meaning of her experience from the inside out rather than imposing meaning on the experience from the outside in. Active empathy means the caregiver is attentively involved in a process of exploration. The companion is trying to grasp what it is like inside the soul—the life force—of the griever.

Empathetic responsiveness requires the ability to go beyond the surface and to become involved in the mourner's feeling world, but always with an "as if" quality of taking another's role without personally experiencing what the other person experiences. What is the inner flavor and what are the unique meanings that the person's experience has for him? What is it that she is trying to express but can't quite say in words?

This empathetic, "bearing witness" process is in contrast to both sympathy and identification. Sympathy is a feeling of concern for someone else without necessarily becoming involved in a close, helping relationship; it projects an "I feel sorry for you" attitude, but stops short of empathy. More destructive than sympathy is identification. This attitude is conveyed by those who submerge themselves with the griever and try to take on their feelings for them. These are people who make assumptions like, "I know just how you feel." The last person the griever feels safe with are those who convey this attitude of over-identification.

"Witness the contents of mind, the visions and sounds, the thoughts, as clouds passing through the vast expanse— the sky-like nature of mind. The rootedness of Being is in emptiness, clarity and awareness: unborn, unspoilt, stainlessly pure." —Alex Grey

Bearing Witness Means Going Beyond "I Know How You Feel"

Bearing witness from a place of active empathy is experienced when the mourner feels you understand. To simply say, "I understand how you feel" is not enough. Empathy is communicated when you, the companion, respond at the emotional, feeling level of the mourner. You reach the mourner where he is, being careful not to bring judgment or a need to get him to "let go" and "move on." This dependable quality of empathy is what seems to free the mourner to open his heart and mourn from the inside out.

Bearing Witness Means Not Trying to "Fix Things"

The more you encourage the mourner to teach you from a position of concerned curiosity, the less you will feel any need to "fix things." As you allow yourself to be taught, you are relieved of any burden to get people where you would like them to go. In other words, you are not attached to outcome.

The paradoxical aspect of this attitude is that the more you allow yourself to be taught and follow the mourner's lead, the more integration of the loss seems to take place. At least this is a very real part of my experience and probably one of the greatest gifts I have discovered in my life's work.

Bearing Witness Means Embracing Feelings of Loss

Observation suggests that some people who attempt to help grieving people hesitate to elicit and embrace feelings such as sadness, loneliness, anxiety and hurt, often fearing that the expression of these feelings at the least "won't do any good," or, at most, will "make matters worse." However, experience suggests that such hesitation is a form of defensive protection for the caregiver who finds it threatening to respond at any true emotional-spiritual level to the mourner.

Just because feelings are threatening does not mean that we as companions should avoid encouraging their expression in the mourner. We should never avoid what a mourner feels because we fear she cannot take it. She is always taking it. The question is whether you will support her in experiencing it with your compassionate presence or only in the isolation of being alone with it. We could also reframe this to note: We as caregivers should never avoid what a mourner implicitly feels because we fear we cannot take it!

Benefits of Bearing Witness Without Bringing Judgment

The capacity to convey active empathy while bearing witness has a number of benefits for the mourner. Among them are the following:

- Empathetic communication is a foundation upon which you establish a companion-witness relationship with the mourner.
- The mourner who feels empathetically understood and not judged is more likely to risk sharing deep, soul-based encounters with grief.
- The mourner's experience of your genuine effort and commitment to understand creates a trusting, low-threat environment that negates the need for self-protection and isolation.
- The communication of empathy encourages self-exploration in the mourner, a prerequisite for compassionate self-understanding and, eventually, movement (with "no rewards for speed") toward reconciliation.

Our choices about attitude related to how to support our fellow human beings in grief often seem to relate to motives and needs. Adopting a bearing-witness-to-the-struggles attitude of "teach me about your grief and I will be with you without judgment" means we give up the status that sometimes falsely comes from being a professional "expert." However, I suspect that in giving up or letting go of some of this ego-based identity, we may well discover our natural compassion.

"The most familiar models of who we are—doctor and patient, 'helper' and 'helped'—often turn out to be major obstacles to the expression of our caring instincts; they limit the full measure of what we have to offer one another... True compassion arises out of unity."—Ram Dass

---

Tenet Six

Companioning is about walking alongside; it is not about leading or being led.

I truly believe that the largest impediment to providing compassionate support to a grieving person is the professional distinction we often make between "us" and "them." Invested in models of separateness, we end up creating distance in the helping relationship. The more you see yourself as having superior knowledge of someone else's grief experience, the more need there is for the griever to play the passive role of being helped.

In my ministry in grief care, I've discovered that true healing lies within the mourner, not the "expert counselor." True compassion evolves when you, the companion, see yourself as a fellow traveler, not as an expert in the mourner's journey. The more you can walk alongside and learn from the mourner, the more you will experience the true grace of an equal relationship of unity.

Another way to think of yourself is as a holder of mirrors. You as grief companion never really "heal" anyone. Instead, you help people heal themselves by holding up mirrors. As they peer into the mirrors, mourners may experience a shift, a transformation of experience anchored in the heart and the soul.

This tenet describes those qualities that I have discovered allow the companion to walk alongside the grieving person. Artful companions are those who keep their hearts open wide and always continue to learn from the true expert—the mourner. If by some chance, your heart has closed off, perhaps the discussion that follows will help you soften and re-open your heart.

This tenet begs the question, "How can we establish a relationship with the mourner that provides a safe environment wherein she feels free to authentically express grief without fear of judgment, isolation or abandonment?" What follows is a brief introduction to the qualities that allow you to walk alongside the mourner. For a separate discussion of the core quality of empathy, see Tenet Five.

Respect

This important quality relates to a nonpossessive caring for and affirmation of the mourner as a separate person capable of healing from the inside out. Respect involves a receptive attitude of having the mourner teach you about her experience of grief. The opposite of this respectful companioning partnership would be the caregiver who presumptuously believes that her superior knowledge of grief qualifies her to project what is best for the mourner to think, feel, and do.

Sensitivity and Warmth

Sensitivity and warmth in the companion are demonstrated through a sense of personal closeness to the mourner as opposed to professional distance. Distancing ourselves from their own or another's pain and acting like they are experts are ways some caregivers get into trouble. Some counselors are even trained to stay professionally distant and come across as cold and impersonal. There is such truth in the saying, "People don't care about how much you know until they know how much you care." Above all, sensitivity and warmth imply patience and the capacity to respond in a nonjudgmental way to the needs of the mourner.

Genuineness

The companion must be truly herself—non-phony and non-defensive. Your words and actions should match your inner feelings. Genuineness results in interpersonal richness. When the mourner senses you are genuine, she can authentically express what is on her heart.

Trust

Trust is about consistency and safety. Grieving people often naturally feel a lack of trust in the world because of the death of someone loved. They sometimes wonder if they should risk trusting or loving again. As a companion, you have an obligation to help the mourner feel consistently safe with you. When trust happens between two people, there is a noticeable exchange of energy. And conversely, when trust is lacking or absent, no energy is exchanged and nothing happens.

Immediacy

This quality has to do with being present to the mourner in the here and now. It goes beyond the content of what is being said to the process of what is happening from moment to moment. The high-functioning companion has the gift of high levels of immediacy. The mourner's needs are right there in the present moment and immediacy allows you to be empathetically responsive to those needs. The present moment is where the needs of the soul reside—and grief work is anchored in soul work.

Humility

This connotes a willingness to learn from one's own mistakes as well as an appreciation of one's limitations and strengths. Humility also means continually being aware of how your own experiences with loss are impacting your presence to the mourner. Helpers who are humble remember to ask questions of themselves such as, "How am I being impacted by sharing in the mourner's experience with grief?"; "Does the mourner's experience with loss remind me of some of my own losses?"; "Where can I share the feelings that supporting this mourner stimulates in me?" Humility means you are not the expert but are open to learning what each new companioning relationship has to teach you about being helpful at this moment in time. And humility interfaces with developing a service ethic—genuinely wanting to care for others, while at the same time realizing you are not "in charge." Instead, you submit yourself to the tenets of companioning (as opposed to treating) and open your soul to the mysterious journey called grief.

Patience

To be patient with the mourner is to let him mourn in his own way and time at a pace he is comfortable with. Some of the deepest communication you may have with a grieving person comes during times of silence and solitude. Being patient is a means of building trust and enhancing the mourner's awareness that you are there to bear witness and learn from his unique experiences. Patience is a very quiet, unassuming quality—the capacity to wait for what is unseen and unspoken to be gradually made manifest. Patience also denotes a quietness of spirit, a deep inner knowing that you will stay present and stand at the mourner's side.

Hope

I believe it is impossible to be a true companion without this quality, for it is in having hope that you communicate your belief that the mourner can and will heal, or "become whole again."

Hope is an expectation of a good that is yet to be. It is an expression of the present alive with a sense of the possible. You create hope in the mourner by having hope in your heart and providing acceptance, recognition, affirmation and gratitude in the context of your helping relationship. Hope rallies energies and activates the courage to commitment of mourning.

Humor

Even in the midst of grief, moments of humor spontaneously occur. How much lighter we feel when we laugh in the midst of our pain. Too much sitting in seriousness violates the laws of the universe.

Heart

To have "heart" as you companion people in grief is to be true to your own feelings, humanness and vulnerabilities. When you work from a place of heart, you function as a whole. When your analytical, thinking self is in charge, you may be just in your head. Yet, the centerpiece of the integration of grief is not the mind, but the heart. Being a companion naturally occurs when you relax into yourself and bring compassion to all of your helping efforts.

This allows you to fulfill not only your personal passion to help those in grief, but also your highest purpose that will be part of your contribution to helping all people mourn well so they can go on to live well and love well. When you minister from the heart, you are in a state of deep connection with the divine, with yourself and with other human beings. You do not minister alone, but in the companionship of other companions.

Once you have explored the ten qualities outlined above, considering your strengths and weaknesses, it is probably best to forget all this and return to this tenet only when you feel that one or more of these qualities is missing in your helping relationships. When you feel yourself struggling in a companioning relationship, you may find that it is because you have temporarily lost touch with one or more of these qualities.

"Do not speak unless you can improve upon silence."
—Buddhist teaching

Tenet Seven

Companioning the bereaved means discovering the gifts of sacred silence; it does not mean filling up every moment with words.

In discovering the gifts of sacred silence, you cultivate what becomes an avenue for the mourner to open his heart up to wisdom surrounding the grief journey. As you quiet yourself, you sustain an open heart and a gentle spirit.

As you focus your every attention on the mourner, you are a source of nourishment. As you companion one person at a time, your compassionate concentration helps quiet the many other potential contenders for your undivided attention.

The Gift of Silence

The mystery of grief has taught me that it requires periods of solitude and silence. The griever may not have access to a cloistered monastery, a walk in the woods, or a stroll on the beach. But, she does have access to your quiet presence and loving spirit. Consciously hush yourself and place trust in the peace you help initiate. Become fully present to another human being who doesn't really need your words but values your soulful presence.

Being silently present to someone in grief requires discernment as to where you channel your energy, your care, your compassion. As you sit with silence, you acknowledge that you value the need to suspend, slow down, and turn inward as part of the grief journey. Giving honor to the instinct to mourn from the inside out requires that we as caregivers come to cherish silence and respect how vital it is to the healing journey.

❖❖❖❖❖❖❖❖❖❖❖❖❖

"Silence is not absence of sound but rather a shifting of attention toward wounds that speak to the soul."
—Thomas Moore

"Non-judgment creates silence of the mind."
—Deepak Chopra

❖❖❖❖❖❖❖❖❖❖❖❖❖

Silence also asks that we respect the role of hurt and pain in healing. If we do not understand this, we will not be capable of silencing our tongues. Instead, we will feel the urge to speak, thinking consciously or unconsciously that we must fix the griever. In so doing, we get in the way of the needed space to initiate the mending of a broken heart. What a gift to come to know the healing power of silence!

Grief Symptoms and Silence

I find it enlightening to explore how it is that many of the symptoms of grief are invitations to the need for silence and solitude. Perhaps the most isolating and frightening part of grief for many people is the sense of disorganization, confusion, searching and yearning that often comes with the loss. As one person noted, "I felt as if I were a lonely traveler with no companion and worse yet, no destination. I could not find myself or anybody else." Yes, the mourner needs silence and solitude.

Another common symptom of grief is the onset of poor judgment-making capabilities. Good judgment is grounded in making choices that are in the best interest of yourself and those for whom you are responsible. Many mourners temporarily lose the capability to make sound judgments. Yes, the mourner needs silence and solitude.

Another common symptom is loss of perspective and a search for meaning. Life naturally seems darker right now than it did otherwise.

Life feels distorted, out of perspective. There are sometimes a multitude of "why" questions to which there are no quick answers. "Why did the person I love have to die now?" "Why should I go on living?" Yes, the mourner needs silence and solitude.

Yet another symptom is the lethargy of grief. Fatigue tries to slow the mourner down and invites a need for privacy. The lethargy that accompanies grief is often more than simply being tired. It reflects that the body's immune system is depleted and that the griever has lost the energy and capacity to respond. The body has such wisdom. Yes, the mourner needs silence and solitude.

"Why did God give man two ears and one mouth? So that he will hear more and talk less."
—Adapted from the Hasdai

The companionship of silence has the ingredients that can bring some peace in the midst of the wilderness. The forces of grief weigh heavy on the heart. Silence serves to lift up the mourner's heart and create much-needed space to give attention to the grief. Being in silence helps restore energy and inspires courage to explore the many facets of transformational grief.

"For many afflictions, silence is the best remedy."
—Talmud

What Silence Can Teach

In choosing to companion instead of treating people in grief, you choose a way of being that values and gives honor to silence. You bring a sensitivity to the importance of listening first. You give attention to the mourner's deepest needs. You acknowledge her uniqueness. You embrace her life force and marry hope to your quiet soul. You silence any instinct to make judgments in your head and you stay connected to your heart. You feel your own emotions as you sit in the stillness and stay in search of a desire to be taught by the mourner. When you do respond, you do it in a considerate and compassionate way that recognizes the vulnerable soul that you are ministering to.

As someone who sits with people in silence, you recognize that so much about grief is a mystery that doesn't lend itself to words. You stand at the graveside with parents who have just experienced the death of their precious child and words are inadequate. You bend down to touch the child whose mother has just died in a tragic auto accident and words are inadequate. The sadness of loss hangs in a wistful silence. Once again you are humbled by an awareness that deep understanding of the ways of life and death cannot be expressed in words.

"Things come suitable to their time."—Enid Bagnold

Tenet Eight

Companioning the bereaved is about being still; it is not about frantic movement forward.

Many of the messages that people in grief are given are in opposition to stillness… "carry on;" "keep your chin up;" "keep busy;" "I have someone for you to meet." Yet, the paradox for many grievers is that as they try to frantically move forward, they often lose their way.

As a companion, your capacity to be still with the mourner will help her honor the deeper voices of quiet wisdom. As Rainer Maria Rilke observed, "Everything is gestation and then bringing forth." In honoring stillness, you help the mourner rest for the journey.

Times of stillness are not anchored in a psychological need but in a spiritual necessity. A lack of stillness hastens confusion and disorientation and results in a waning of the spirit. If the mourner does not rest in stillness, she cannot and will not find her way out of the wilderness of grief. Stillness allows for movement from soul work to spirit work; it restores the life force.

"There is more to life than merely increasing its speed."—Gandhi

Within the sanctuary of stillness, discernment that is bathed in grace and wisdom is born. Thus, one of my mantras as a caregiver is, "Go slow; there are no rewards for speed." Grief is only transformed when we honor the quiet forces of stillness.

Without Stillness

Without stillness the mourner cannot create the energy needed to embrace the work of mourning. In sitting with suffering in stillness, you make yourself available for those you companion to give voice to their grief. You become present to the insight and wisdom that comes forth only out of stillness. It's as if the stillness invites the head to settle gently in the heart.

Without stillness, the mourner lacks a foundation from which to, eventually, transform grief into renewed meaning and purpose. The mourner needs stillness to encounter the full force of the powerful nature of grief. Out of the stillness often comes the inspiration to be respectful of grief, to seek the wisdom of those who have gone before.

Observation has taught me that the integration of grief is borne out of stillness, not frantic movement forward. By saying no to the use of techniques to try to "make something happen," sacred space arises for things to happen; Divine Momentum is set in motion. When we stop managing grief, other things such as grace, wisdom, love and truth come forth.

In honoring stillness as a companion to someone in grief, you discover that spiritual forces evolve that discourage striving and encourage rest and eventual renewal. Attempting to consciously move forward, or worse yet, making any attempt to get him to "let go," becomes counterproductive. Frantic movement forward depletes an already naturally malnourished soul. It is through stillness that one's soul is ever so slowly restored.

◇-◇-◇-◇-◇-◇-◇-◇-◇-◇-◇-◇-◇-◇

"The rhythm of stillness is the teacher of contentment and peace."
—Gabriella Roth

"The wounds of the past must be tended by more than the frantic activity of 'getting on with it.'"
—Oriah Mountain Dreamer

◇-◇-◇-◇-◇-◇-◇-◇-◇-◇-◇-◇-◇-◇

Stillness and Pain

As a companion, you will be well served to focus your heart's attention on the importance of stillness in relation to pain and suffering. If you do not perceive value in the role of pain in healing it will be all but impossible to be still with people in grief.

If you in any way perceive the pain of grief as unnecessary or inappropriate, you will be reluctant to be in the stillness. In stillness, you come face to face with the essence of grief and raw feelings of loss and profound sadness. At times, you will confront the dark night of the soul—a profound sense of spiritual deprivation wherein the person you are companioning may well question the very desire to go on living.

"I learned the interior life was as rewarding as the exterior life and that my richest moments occurred when I was absolutely still."
—Richard Bode

If you do not see that it is in hurting that we ultimately heal, you will greet stillness with anxiety and fear. Fearful of what you might find in the stillness, you will instinctually push stillness away, keeping yourself and the mourner busy with techniques intended to avoid the depth of a multitude of feelings. In stillness, as you stop and listen, you will hear and feel the emptiness that accompanies grief.

"I never found a companion that was as companionable as solitude."
—Henry David Thoreau

By contrast, if you surrender to the reality that pain and suffering are part of the healing journey, you can sit with the stillness. You can step back from any urge to fix the pain. You can appreciate and trust that out of the darkness will eventually come the light. You will see the underlying strength and wisdom that is borne out of respect for the stillness. You will come to see that it is out of the stillness that the person discovers that authentic mourning invites the blessings of living fully each and every day.

"Instead of struggling against the force of confusion, we could meet it and relax."—Pema Chodron

---

Tenet Nine

Companioning is about respecting disorder and confusion; it is not about imposing order and logic.

The death of someone loved brings about significant change in the life of the mourner. Change of any kind starts with disorder and confusion. Companioning is not about understanding the disorder and confusion, figuring it out, or trying to make it better.

The challenge for the companion is to stay present to the disorientation, and trust that the natural unfolding process will eventually result in re-orientation. When it comes to matters of the soul, the last thing the mourner needs is to be joined at the head level. When disoriented and confused, he needs companions at the heart level. If you can give up the hope that disorder and confusion can be quickly and efficiently moved away from, then you can help the mourner be more self-compassionate and not feel such urging to be rid of these normal symptoms of the journey.

❖❖❖❖❖❖❖❖❖❖❖❖❖❖

"A deep distress has humanized my soul."
—William Wordsworth

❖❖❖❖❖❖❖❖❖❖❖❖❖❖

The Disorder of Grief

Disorder and confusion is a time of waiting, a time of paralysis, a time when the world doesn't make sense in the way it did before the death.

The mourner may experience a sense of restlessness, agitation, impatience, and ongoing confusion. There is often an inability to complete tasks. The mourner is often forgetful and everyday pleasures may not seem to matter right now.

✧✧✧✧✧✧✧✧✧✧✧✧✧

"I wanted a perfect ending. Now I've learned, the hard way, that some poems don't rhyme, and some stories don't have a clear beginning, middle, and end. Life is about not knowing, having to change, taking the moment and making the best of it, without knowing what's going to happen next. Delicious Ambiguity."—Gilda Radner

✧✧✧✧✧✧✧✧✧✧✧✧✧

The mourner may experience a restless searching for the person who died. This searching and yearning can leave her feeling drained and can be accompanied by the "lethargy of grief." These are only a few of many care-eliciting symptoms the mourner may have when experiencing disorder and confusion.

The unfortunate reality is that many grievers do not give themselves permission to surrender to or relax into their disorder and confusion. We live in a society that often encourages the repression or denial of any kind of disorder and confusion, and in its place we impose order and logic: "You just need to get ahold of yourself and get on with life. Being upset isn't going to change anything." The result of this is that many people either grieve in isolation or attempt to run away from their grief through various means, including order and logic.

Using Logic to Order Grief

While there are a number of unique ways by which people repress, deny, or move away from the disorienting symptoms of grief, I will limit my discussion here to the minimizer/intellectualizer who tries to use order and logic to overcome grief. This person is usually very sensitive to feelings of disorder and confusion, but when he feels them works to minimize them by diluting them through a variety of rationalizations.

This person often attempts to prove to himself that he is not really impacted by the loss. Observers of the minimizer/intellectualizer may hear him talk about how well he is doing and how he is back to his normal routine. On a conscious level his logic may seem to be working and certainly conforms to society's message to quickly "get over" one's grief. However, internally the repressed feelings of grief build and emotional and spiritual strain—soul symptoms—result.

This person often believes (often because of unconscious contamination by a mourning-avoidant culture) that grief is something to be thought through but not felt through. This is typically an intellectual process in which words become a substitute for the expression of authentic feelings. Any disorder and confusion is threatening to the minimizer/intellectualizer, who seeks to avoid feeling a loss of control. Worse yet, she might find an "expert" counselor who shares these beliefs and tries to use techniques to overcome the disorder and confusion.

❖◦❖◦❖◦❖◦❖◦❖◦❖◦❖◦❖◦❖◦❖◦❖

"The truth is that our finest moments are most likely to occur when we are feeling deeply uncomfortable, unhappy, or unfulfilled. For it is only in such moments, propelled by our discomfort, that we are likely to step out of our ruts and start searching for different ways or truer answers."
—M. Scott Peck

❖◦❖◦❖◦❖◦❖◦❖◦❖◦❖◦❖◦❖◦❖◦❖

Unfortunately, the more this person works to convince herself that the feelings of grief have been overcome, the more crippled she becomes in allowing for emotional and spiritual expression. The result is often a destructive, vicious cycle.

In my experience, the need for the mourner to stay logical and orderly are usually problems in allowing oneself to feel and express deep feelings. Some people struggle with a high need for self-control, others may have an intolerance for experiences of disorder and confusion accompanied by pain and helplessness, while still others may lack a support system that encourages the expression of their feelings.

Yes, the disorder and confusion that accompany grief can be overwhelming to the mourner. When she is encountering this disorientation, everything in her may want to shut down. Yet, in the process she may be tempted to shut out precisely what she needs. She may see the disorder and confusion as the enemy.

As a companion, you, on the other hand, realize that there is no enemy and that these symptoms are the result of being torn apart by grief. The disorder is a biofeedback mechanism reminding the mourner to stay open to the loss. Now, the question becomes: how will she host the disorder and confusion? Will she try to will it away through order and logic, or will she be patient, self-nurturing and seek the support of compassionate companions?

Without doubt, one of the reasons many people are preoccupied with the question, "How long does grief last?" has to do with society's impatience with grief. Persons who continue to express grief are often viewed as "weak," "crazy" or "self-pitying." Grief is something to be overcome instead of experienced.

The result of these kinds of messages is to encounter the adoption of rational, mechanistic principles of order and logic to defend against disorder and confusion. Refusal to allow tears, suffering in silence and "being strong" are thought to be admirable behaviors. Yet, the most helpful approach to grief is to approach it head-on and honor the value of symptoms that reflect special needs.

❖❖❖❖❖❖❖❖❖❖❖❖❖❖❖❖❖❖❖❖❖❖❖❖❖❖❖❖❖❖❖

"Have patience with everything that remains unsolved in your heart. Try to love the questions themselves, like locked rooms and like books written in a foreign language. Do not now look for the answers. They cannot now be given to you because you could not live them. It is a question of experiencing everything. At present you need to live the question. Perhaps you will gradually, without even noticing it, find yourself experiencing the answer, some distant day."—Rainer Maria Rilke

❖❖❖❖❖❖❖❖❖❖❖❖❖❖❖❖❖❖❖❖❖❖❖❖❖❖❖❖❖❖❖

The Silent Mourner

The lack of expression of outward mourning has brought about the evolution of the "silent mourner." Even persons who want to be supportive cannot identify this mourner. The relegating of grief to behind closed doors reinforces the importance of being outreach-oriented in your companioning efforts.

All too often, our society fails to support mourners who suffer from soul-based symptoms of disorder and confusion. An emphasis on being rational and under control influences the mourner to reintegrate into the social network and keep their tears, fears, and pains to themselves. As a responsible rebel, I invite you to join me in an effort to reverse this trend that fails to acknowledge the need for compassion and support to people who experience normal symptoms of disorder and confusion of grief. Supporting people in grief is about love; it is not about logic!

Tenet Ten

Companioning is about learning from others; it is not about teaching them.

When I attended graduate school in traditional psychology, I learned semantics such as *assess, diagnose* and *treat*. In large part, I was taught to study a body of knowledge surrounding mental health, assume expert status as a professional, and treat people as patients. Yes, I was taught a catalog of disorders and standard interventions based on the assumption that I had made an accurate diagnosis. What I later came to call my "unconscious contamination" had me believing I was responsible for the cure. It was only through time, maturation and experience that I came to reject this model of caregiving.

Walking with thousands of people in grief has resulted in an "educated heart" that has led me to accept my role as a responsible rebel. I learned the medical model of mental health care, but my real life experiences caused me to reject it in favor of a companioning model of caregiving. As I noted in the Introduction, I believe that our modern understanding of grief lacks an appreciation for and attention to the spiritual, soulful nature of the grief journey.

I have left my clinical doctoring behind to become the companion I am today. As a companion, I believe that grief is organic. Grief is as natural as the setting of the sun and as elemental as gravity. Grief is a complex but perfectly natural—and necessary—mixture of human emotions. Companions do not cure mourners; instead we create conditions that allow them to teach us. Our ministry is more art than science, more head than heart. The bereaved person is not our patient but instead our companion.

Support Groups and Stories

In North America today, thousands of people find this kind of companionship in grief support groups. The worth of these programs certainly does not emanate from empirically supported treatments, but from something much more simple (yet powerful): the telling of stories. The meetings are anchored in honoring each member's stories of grief and supporting each other's need to authentically mourn. No effort is made to interpret or analyze. The group affirms the storyteller for the courage to express the raw wounds that often accompany loss. The stories speak the truth. The stories create hope. The stories create healing.

> *"Healers are hosts who patiently and carefully listen to the story of the suffering strangers."* —Henri Nouwen

Effective leaders of such groups come to recognize that their role is not so much about group counseling techniques as it is about creating "sacred space" in the group so that each person's story can be non-judgmentally received. Effective grief group leadership is a humble yet demanding role of creating this space in ways that members can express their wounds in the body of community. The very experience of telling one's story in the common bond of the group contradicts the isolation and shame that characterizes so many people's lives in a mourning-avoidant culture. And, because stories of love and loss take time, patience, and unconditional love, they serve as powerful antidotes to a modern society that is all too often preoccupied with getting people to "let go" and "move on."

> *"Stories, carefully chosen and shaped by both the teller and the listener, can open gateways into our interior landscape, can reveal the meaning in our lives enfolded in the details and unfolded in their telling and conscious contemplation."*
> —Oriah Mountain Dreamer

The creation of new meaning and purpose in life requires that mourners "re-story" their lives. Obviously, this calls out for the need for empathetic companions, not treaters. Indigenous cultures acknowledge that honoring stories helps reshape a person's experience. The stories are re-shaped not in the telling of the story once or twice or even three times, but over and over again. Mourners need compassionate listeners to hear and affirm their truths. So, as a companion, your upholding of people's stories allows you the privilege of being a "shapeshifter!"

The many benefits of honoring the stories of our fellow human beings include:

- We can search for wholeness among our fractured parts.
- We can come to know who we are in new and unexpected ways.
- We can explore our past and come to a more profound understanding of our origins and our future directions.
- We can tentatively explain our view of the world and come to understand who we are.
- We can explore how love experienced and love lost have influenced our time on earth.
- We can discover that a life without story is like a book without pages—nice to see but lacking in substance.
- We can seek forgiveness and be humbled by our mortality.
- We can determine how adversity has enriched our meaning and purpose in life.
- We can journey inward and discover connections previously not understood or acknowledged.
- We can create an awareness of how the past interfaces with the present, and how the present ebbs back into the past.
- We can discover that the route to healing lies not only in the physical realm, but also in the emotional and spiritual realms.
- We can find that the fulfillment of a life well lived is bestowed through the translation of our past into experiences that are expressed through the oral or written word.
- We can realize that the true significance of each unique story is that you can capture the spirit, the soul, and the genuine worth of the person who has died.
- We can come to understand that in our pain and suffering lies the awareness of the preciousness of each day on the earth.
- We can discover our truth in this present moment of time and space.

Honoring Our Own Stories

I believe that mourners can instinctively sense who can listen to their stories and who cannot. They often look for signs of open-heartedness and will gladly tell their stories to those they sense have a receptive spirit. The capacity to attend to your own stories of loss allows you to open your heart and connect to other people's stories.

Honoring stories, both our own and others', requires that we slow down, turn inward and create the sacred space to do so. Yes, this can be challenging in a fast-paced, efficiency-based culture in which many people lack an understanding of the value of telling the story.

Yet, companions realize that it is in having places to re-story their lives that they can embrace what needs to be embraced and come to understand that the human spirit prevails. We heal ourselves as we tell the tale. This is the awesome power of the story.

❖❖❖❖❖❖❖❖❖❖❖❖❖❖❖❖❖❖❖

"Telling a story, especially about ourselves, can be one of the most personal and intimate things we can do."—Richard Stone

❖❖❖❖❖❖❖❖❖❖❖❖❖❖❖❖❖❖❖

Tenet Eleven

Companioning is about curiosity; it is not about expertise.

Curiosity for the companion is about being willing to enter into and learn about the mystery of grief while recognizing you do not and cannot fully understand someone else's experience. Curiosity is bathed in an attitude that Zen calls the "beginner's mind" or "know-nothing mind."

This attitude is not ignorance but the capacity to see without assumptions, to take a fresh look each and every time you are privileged to walk with and learn from a mourner. It involves a clearing away of thoughts, beliefs, and ideas that might cloud your ability to see things as they are in pristine form.

As we all realize, children are naturally curious. As we grow up we are at risk for losing this state of heightened awareness and natural desire to learn from those around us. We may falsely assume we already

❖❖❖❖❖❖❖❖❖❖❖❖❖❖❖❖❖❖❖❖❖❖❖❖❖❖❖❖❖❖❖

"Listening for and being curious about client competencies, resources, and resiliencies does not mean that the therapist ignores the client's pain or assumes a cheerleading attitude. Rather, it requires that the therapist listen to the whole story; the confusion and the clarity, the suffering and the endurance, the pain and the coping, the desperation, and the desire."
—From *The Heroic Client*, by Barry Duncan and Scott Miller

❖❖❖❖❖❖❖❖❖❖❖❖❖❖❖❖❖❖❖❖❖❖❖❖❖❖❖❖❖❖❖

know. In other words, our intellect takes over. Yet, being a companion to people in grief can reactivate our sense of miracle to bring a fresh, simple, unsophisticated view of things.

You Don't Know

Paradoxically, you can only learn from the mourner by acknowledging you don't know. It is out of your helplessness that you ultimately become helpful. You have to be willing to disconnect from believing you have superior expertise of another human being's emotional-spiritual journey of grief.

Through no fault of your own, your training as a caregiver may make it difficult to admit you don't know and don't have answers. You may instinctively be frightened to be present to people that are in liminal space—betwixt and between!

❖❖❖❖❖❖❖❖❖❖❖❖❖

"Communities of like-minded people develop beliefs and practices, teach them to each other, reinforce them as the standard beliefs of the community, and lose sight of the fact that those beliefs and practices are their own make-do creations."
—Robert T. Fancher

❖❖❖❖❖❖❖❖❖❖❖❖❖

Actually, you may have been taught that part of being a professional is to project confidence and to state opinions as if they were gospel. You don't get respected in this culture by admitting you are confused or by asking tentative questions in search of enhancing your empathy versus providing techniques for brief therapy that collaborates with managed care. The unconscious contamination of your training is more likely to encourage you to assess, diagnose, and treat than it is to observe, witness, listen, learn, and watch out for the mourner.

For some caregivers it is difficult, if not impossible, to relinquish their "diagnostic categories," "interventions," and "treatments." These terms often lie at the heart of the professional identity of the caregiver and the attempt to be part of the medical model of expertise. Yet, the companion humbly acknowledges that "compassionate curiosity" is what you really need to care for the mourner.

You have the honor as a companion to listen and to learn, to be curious rather than to be certain. The greatest privilege of the companioning model, in fact, is that it moves you closer to the very people you wish to support. When you listen without a need to judge or interpret, you create a safe place and become a safe person for the mourner.

At bottom, it is not differences that divide us. Instead, it is our judgments about each other that do. Curiosity and use of the "teach me" model bring us back together. To use this model invites us to rest in the sometimes uncomfortable place of uncertainty of not knowing, having the answer, or being the expert. Companioning invites you to pay attention to the soul work and spirit work and to be led rather than to lead.

❖❖❖❖❖❖❖❖❖❖❖❖❖❖

Compassionate curiosity

Actively encouraging the mourner to teach you about her grief while you remain patient, humble and caring.

❖❖❖❖❖❖❖❖❖❖❖❖❖❖

The Myth of the Expert

Today, more and more caregivers are seeking certification as grief educators, counselors, and therapists. My own Center for Loss and Life Transition offers a certificate in Death and Grief Studies. Yet I want to be clear that the receiving of this certificate following 150 hours of reflection on the mystery of death and grief doesn't make the recipient an expert. Actually, it means the person has been willing to ponder the mysteries and learn to be curious when learning from the true expert—the mourner! To be perceived, or worse yet, to perceive oneself, as an expert grief counselor may be the first step toward unbecoming a creative companion.

A Buddhist teaching notes, "In the beginner's mind there are many possibilities; in the expert's mind there are few." One astute observer of this reality was Bradford Keeney, who wrote the following about the hazards of being an expert or master counselor: "You will find that it no longer matters what you say. Everything uttered will be contextualized as the voice of a master... Avoid the political posturings of 'mastery' and return to embracing and cultivating a beginner's mind. Maintain and respect ignorance. Speak to hear the surprise from your own voice."

❖❖❖❖❖❖❖❖❖❖❖❖

"The great danger of the increasing professionalization of the different forms of healing is that they become ways of exercising power instead of offering service."

—Henri Nouwen

❖❖❖❖❖❖❖❖❖❖❖❖

As you contemplate the value of curiosity versus expertise, listen to your own inner voice. What has your own personal grief taught you about what helps people heal? Have you witnessed change as the journey unfolds, but not according to plan or as a consequence of intentional intervention? Do you appreciate the mystery of grief and challenge the wish to have it resolved (which it can never be)? Do you believe that caring for the mourner requires a different language than that of modern academic psychology? Depending on your answers, you may have to admit you are a responsible rebel who believes in compassionate curiosity and challenges ego-based expertise.

I believe that every counselor must work to develop his or her own theory or point of view about what helps bereaved people heal. Challenging yourself to explain what happens in your counseling relationships with bereaved people and families will, in my experience, assist you in understanding and improving the work you do to assist those you desire to companion.

Developing your own tenets encourages a coherence of ideas about the helping process and generates new ideas about how to be helpful. Now that you've read about my tenets of companioning the bereaved, I hope you will give thought to yours. I encourage you to spend a few moments jotting down some ideas before you begin reading Part Two.

Part Two

From Philosophy to Practice:
Wisdom Teachings for
Companioning

"Not only does the counselor's view of grief change through the lens of 'companioning,' but the approach to counseling/supporting our fellow human beings is transformed as well."—Alan D. Wolfelt

---

Putting compassion into action

My sincere hope is that the information explored in Part Two of this resource will serve as a source of encouragement and practical help to those who seek an understandable framework for moving from philosophy to practice in the art of companioning the bereaved. A major purpose of this section of the book is to inspire you to put your care and compassion into action.

As you explored Part One of this book, I trust that you discovered I believe that grief is not an affliction to be "treated," a crisis to be "resolved," "closure" to be had, or an experience to be "overcome." I trust you discovered I believe that what the death of someone precious calls out for is not to be "explained," but to be expressed and storied gently over time, and in small doses, to find its way to meaning.

The companioning philosophy of grief care becomes a collaborative journey—a helping alliance—that facilitates authentic mourning and the survivor's search for meaning. The helping process becomes one of discovery instead of recovery. Responses to loss are valued and understood in the context of a soul-stirring, life-changing experience. Symptoms reflecting the wounds of grief become messengers for underlying needs.

Worldview: The set of beliefs people have about how the universe functions and what place they, as individuals, occupy therein.

In embracing this philosophy, the counselor is the companion who is willing to be taught. There is no "resolution wish" (see page 7) but rather an understanding of the concepts of "not attached to outcome," "no rewards for speed," and "Divine Momentum." There is a shared understanding that the death of someone precious is a life-altering experience that will be felt throughout the survivor's lifetime and results in a changed worldview.

There is a recognition that when the mourner's worldview becomes vulnerable, she often needs long-term support in reconstruction prior to becoming more fully engaged in life, living and loving. She is literally "under reconstruction."

Yet, even while there is a natural reconstruction process being experienced, the companioning model is grounded in honoring a renewed sense of hope. In fact, hope is the foundation of the companioning model. Hope is an expectation of a good that is yet to be. It is an expression of the present alive with a sense of the possible. It is a belief that healing can and will occur. Companioning is the art of sus-

❖❖❖❖❖❖❖❖❖❖❖❖❖❖❖❖❖❖❖❖❖❖❖❖❖❖❖❖❖❖❖❖

What is healing in grief?

To heal in grief is to become whole again, to integrate your grief into your self and to learn to continue your changed life with fullness and meaning. Experiencing a new and changed "wholeness" requires that you engage in the work of mourning. It doesn't happen to you; you must stay open to that which has broken you.

Healing is a holistic concept that embraces the physical, emotional, cognitive, social and spiritual realms. Note that healing is not the same as curing, which is a medical term that means "remedying" or "correcting." You cannot remedy your grief, but you can reconcile it. You cannot correct your grief, but you can heal it.

Healing

…is encountering what is most feared.
…is opening to what it might be tempting to close oneself off from.
…is coming in tune with truth, integrating the reality of the death
   and embracing the pain of the loss.
…is a never-ending journey into wholeness.
…is honoring the past while hoping for the future.
…is about exploring the transformation of the heart and soul.
…is not being attached to outcome and bathing in Divine
   Momentum.

❖❖❖❖❖❖❖❖❖❖❖❖❖❖❖❖❖❖❖❖❖❖❖❖❖❖❖❖❖❖❖❖

taining the presence of hope as the mourner feels separated from those things that make life worth living. Companioning is the recognition that suffering must be affirmed before it can be transcended.

The Art of Observance

To care for people in grief, you must create a safe, sacred space for people to gently embrace their feelings of loss. This safe place is a cleared-out compassionate heart that starts with observance. The concept of observance comes to us from ritual and ceremony. It means "to watch out for," "to keep and honor," "to bear witness." To care for and about grieving people is to nurture souls as they actively mourn.

These principles of "to watch out for," "to keep and honor" and "to bear witness," in turn, are all about the art of sitting with and being totally present to human suffering, to embrace it for what it is, to not run from it. When you "watch out for," you turn toward the sufferer and invite her experience to enter your heart. Creating this sacred space does not make the suffering go away. By contrast, it often naturally intensifies feelings on the path toward healing. You cannot cure the human experience of grief, but you can create a free and open space for the mourner. You can turn away from grief and loss, or you can turn toward grief and loss. Those are your two choices. True companions consciously choose the later.

To assist you in consciously turning toward grief and loss and transitioning from philosophy to practice, I will now explore some of the "wisdom teachings" that mourners have taught me. Essentially, the content that follows is what I have come to believe that we as companions need to watch out for, keep and honor, and bear witness to as we are enriched by the companioning experience.

These wisdom teachings are explained in five chapters. First you will find a brief overview of some misconceptions about grief and mourning. Providing compassionate care to grieving people demands an understanding of these misconceptions. Second, you will be asked to ponder the unique influences on the mourner's journey into grief.

This foundational overview provides some insight into the "whys" of each mourner's unique response to death loss and suggests some important questions you can ask yourself about these influences as you learn from the mourner. Next, we will explore a multitude of common responses in the mourner and learn ways to be a heart-centered companion in response to the needs of the unique person. This is followed by an overview of my perception of six central needs of mourning and the importance of creating hospitality for the mourner to "dose" herself on these needs. A closing section provides a look into the transformative nature of grief.

> "Spiritual intelligence requires a particular kind of emptiness, a sophisticated ignorance, an increasing ability to forget what you know and to give up the need to understand."
>
> —Thomas Moore

Clearly, no one book—not this book, not any book—can tell us everything there is to know about death and grief. Actually the more we think we know, or the more we believe we are experts, the more we will probably be humbled by our own personal experiences with loss. We can probably never know as much as we might like to about grief, but in knowing what we don't know we can be open to the mystery.

The paradox of wisdom is knowing we don't ever arrive and get anointed (or worse yet, anoint ourselves) as master grief counselors. Entering into the mystery is to learn from the mourner and stand in the wonder. While mysterious teachings do not provide you an exact script of what to say and do to give care to mourners, I hope that exploring the following wisdom teachings will encourage you to balance your knowledge with your heart and soul. Free of the illusion that knowledge brings mastery, you can explore your compassionate curiosity; you allow the mourner to be your teacher, not the other way around. Perhaps it is through fostering our human capacity to stay open to the mystery of grief that we can continue to enrich each moment of our living. May you find inspiration and hope in the pages that follow.

Wisdom Teaching One:
Be Aware of Common
Misconceptions About Grief

I have discovered that an important wisdom teaching for those who companion mourners and their families is to provide a brief overview of some misconceptions surrounding grief and mourning. For some readers of this text, some of these misconceptions may seem basic or be something you are already aware of. If so, forgive me; however, I have decided not to make the assumption that every reader is familiar with this foundational information.

Providing heart-centered care to grieving people requires an understanding of these misconceptions. Don't condemn yourself or others if, as you read this section, you find that you have internalized some of these misconceptions. Instead, make use of any new insights to enhance your care of those people you are privileged to help.

Misconception 1:
Grief and mourning are the same thing.

An excellent starting point in attempting to provide a framework to the art of companioning is to simply make some semantic distinctions in commonly used terms. However, in doing so, we should acknowledge that words are inadequate in conveying the magnitude of these experiences.

Grief and *mourning* are terms that do not mean precisely the same thing, although most people (including counselors) use them interchangeably. However, there is a critical distinction that you as companion must be aware of. We as humans move toward integrating loss into our lives not just by grieving, but by mourning.

Grief is the constellation of internal thoughts and feelings you experience within yourself about a loss. Grief is the internal meaning given to the external event.

Mourning is the outward expression of grief, or "grief gone public." Crying, talking about the person who died, journaling and acknowledging special anniversary dates are only a few examples of mourning. The specific ways in which people mourn are influenced in numerous ways, including unique personality, family of origin and ethnic and cultural background. There is no one "right way" to mourn and the companion is always respectful of this reality.

❖❖❖❖❖❖❖❖❖❖❖❖❖

Bereavement is a state caused by loss such as death. It means "to be torn apart," "to have special needs," "to be robbed."

❖❖❖❖❖❖❖❖❖❖❖❖❖

We should note that the mourning behavior expressed may not be in agreement with true feelings of the bereaved. Why? Because the person may experience disapproval if they do not follow family rules or prescribed social customs.

A major theme of this book is rooted in the importance of openly and honestly mourning life losses. A critical part of the helping role of the companion is to create safe, sacred space for the bereaved person and family to express grief outwardly and without shame. Over time and with the support of compassionate companions, to mourn is to integrate loss into life.

Interesting to note is that many native cultures actually created vessels – usually baskets, pots, or bowls – that symbolically contained their grief. They would put these vessels away for periods of time, only to bring them out on a regular basis to help themselves mourn.

Another way to think about what these cultures were instinctively doing was dosing themselves with their grief. They embraced their grief and converted it to mourning little by little, in small bits with breaks in between. This dosing helped them survive what would, if absorbed in its totality all at once, overwhelm them.

When a death loss is not given the attention it deserves by acknowledging it, first to oneself and then to those around you, the grief accumulates. Then, the denied losses come flowing out in all sorts of potential ways that I refer to as "living in the shadow of the ghosts" (e.g., deep depression, physical complaints, difficulty in relationships, addictive behaviors), compounding the pain of the loss.

> *"Eighty percent of our life is emotion, and only twenty percent is intellect. I am much more interested in how you feel than how you think."* —Frank Luntz

Obviously, bereavement, grief and mourning are much more than these semantic distinctions. Grief and mourning are real and they do not simply go away as time passes. Experiencing grief and mourning is often movement through an unfamiliar territory that is embraced by an overwhelming sense of pain and loss. And yet, helping people turn toward their grief and find avenues for expression of authentic mourning allows the companion to be a catalyst for healing.

Misconception 2:
There are predictable, orderly stages to grief and mourning.

Most caregivers are familiar with the concept of "stages of grief." The notion of stages helps people try to make logical sense of a journey that is usually not orderly or predictable. If you were to believe that everyone grieves/mourns by going through the same stages, then the experience of loss becomes more manageable and less mysterious. If only it were so simple!

"Stages" of grief were popularized in 1969 with the publication of Elizabeth Kubler-Ross's landmark text *On Death and Dying*. In her book, Dr. Kubler-Ross noted five stages of grief that she observed terminally ill persons encounter in the face of their own impending death: denial, anger, bargaining, depression, and acceptance. However, she never intended for her perception of these stages to be literally interpreted as a rigid, linear sequence to be prescribed to all mourners. Some caregivers, however, have done just that and the results have been that many mourners have been prescribed what they should experience instead of encouraged to teach what they do experience. Obviously, this is the total opposite of a teach-me, companioning model.

◇◇◇◇◇◇◇◇◇◇◇◇◇◇

"We have to find ways to unlearn those things that screen us from the perception of profound truth."
—Thomas Moore

◇◇◇◇◇◇◇◇◇◇◇◇◇◇

This misconception is a reminder that each person mourns in different ways. As a companion you do not try to move anyone through prescribed stages of grief. You do have an obligation to become familiar with "Dimensions of Response" (see Wisdom Teaching Three) and how to be a responsive witness to the unfolding journey.

A major premise of the companioning model is that each person's grief is unique. Actually, the word unique means "only one." A central element of this integration of grief into one's life is this truth: the thoughts and feelings experienced must be respected as unique and essential to each person.

Misconception 3:
We should avoid the painful parts
of the grief experience.

As noted throughout Part One of this book, our society often encourages prematurely moving away from grief instead of toward it. The result is that too many bereaved people either grieve in isolation, self-treat the pain, or run away from their grief. Through no conscious fault of their own, far too many people view grief as something to be overcome rather than experienced. When people either grieve without mourning, self-treat their pain, or run from their grief, they ultimately avoid moving toward reconciliation of the death.

In many ways, and as strange as it may seem to some, the role of the companion is to help people honor the pain that grief brings. Honoring means recognizing the value of and respecting. In a mourning-avoidant culture, it is not instinctive for people to see the need to openly mourn as something to honor, yet the capacity to love requires the necessity to mourn. To honor one's grief is not self-destructive or harmful, it is self-sustaining and life-giving!

The pain of grief will keep trying to get the griever's attention until she has the courage to gently, and in small doses, open to its presence. The alternative —moving away from the pain of grief—is in fact more painful. Walking with and learning from thousands of people in grief and experiencing my own losses has taught me that the pain that surrounds the closed heart of grief is the pain of living against oneself, the pain of denying how loss changes you, the pain of feeling alone and isolated—unable to openly mourn, unable to love and be loved by those around you.

"There is no coming to consciousness without pain." —Carl Jung

Instead of collaborating with those people who believe that closing to the pain is the answer, as a companion you work to create sacred space to open to the presence of the loss. As an ancient Hebrew sage observed, "If you want life, you must expect suffering." Paradoxically, as you "bear witness" to the pain that loss naturally initiates, you help the mourner stay present (in doses) to her wounded heart and commit herself to authentic mourning. In your willingness to "be with" her, you are helping her find her way into and through the wilderness of her grief and find and give attention to those places that need to be healed.

"We are healed of a suffering only by experiencing it in the full." —Marcel Proust

A caveat: not everyone around you will understand this "opening to the presence of the loss." Many of the techniques that surround grief "management" forget that mourners must always say hello before they say goodbye. So, remember to be the "responsible rebel" you are and recognize the value of affirming the pain before thinking your helping role is to get the mourner to efficiently transcend the pain.

Misconception 4:
Tears of grief are a sign of weakness.

You will probably discover that many mourners are at risk for having internalized this misconception. Just recently, there was an obituary in my local newspaper that reinforces this misconception. The content described a man who had done many things in life, had many friends, and had touched the lives of countless people. He died in his 60s of cancer. At the end of the obituary, readers were invited to attend his funeral service and were instructed to bring memories and stories, but no TEARS.

Beyond this one example, I often have people come to the Center for Loss and Life Transition and as they begin to tell their story, tears naturally begin to flow. Almost without exception this is followed by an apology for crying. Of course, my thought is that if you can't cry at the Center for Loss, where can you cry?

Obviously, when you discover in your helping role that the mourner has internalized this misconception, part of your efforts to support her demand some gentle education about how tears are a lovely expression of mourning. You can help her understand that comments she may receive from others, such as "Tears won't bring him back" or "He wouldn't want you to cry," are usually well intended, but misinformed. In contrast, you can help the mourner affirm that crying is nature's way of releasing internal tension in her body and allows her to communicate a need to be comforted.

❖❖❖❖❖❖❖❖❖❖❖❖❖❖❖❖❖❖❖❖❖❖❖❖❖❖❖❖❖❖

"There is a sacredness in tears. They are not the mark of weakness, but of power. They speak more eloquently than ten thousand tongues. They are messengers of overwhelming grief...and unspeakable love." —Washington Irving

❖❖❖❖❖❖❖❖❖❖❖❖❖❖❖❖❖❖❖❖❖❖❖❖❖❖❖❖❖❖

As a companion it will also make sense to you that suppressing tears that need expression can also increase susceptibility to a multitude of stress-related disorders. Upon reflection, this makes good common sense. Crying is one of the excretory processes. Perhaps like sweating and exhaling, crying helps remove waste products from the body.

If your experience fits with mine, you will be likely to also observe a change in physical appearance after a mourner cries. Apparently, not only do people feel better after they cry, they also seem to look better. Tension and agitation seem to flow out of their bodies.

❖❖❖❖❖❖❖❖❖❖❖❖❖

"Let my hidden weeping arise and blossom."
—Rainer Maria Rilke

❖❖❖❖❖❖❖❖❖❖❖❖❖

Your helping role is anchored in helping mourners be self-compassionate about their tears, to recognize authentic crying is not a sign of weakness or inadequacy. In fact, the capacity to express tears is an indication of a willingness to actively mourn life losses.

Do keep in mind that some people have never been criers, and there should be no shame around that reality. Tears are only one of many avenues to mourn. A compassionate caregiver never forces tears, but is responsibly supportive when they are part of the mourner's experience.

Another important learning I have had surrounding tears is that many mourners value the caregiver's supportive presence as they explore the meaning of their tears. The meaning of tears often changes as the grief experience unfolds. Whereas early in grief tears might be expressive of acute pain resulting from the loss, at another time tears may be expressive of the joy of having the opportunity to embrace memories of the person who died.

The companion resists the urge to directly interpret the meaning of tears for the mourner; however, you can create space for silence, personal reflection, and a supportive presence that quietly encourages the mourner to provide her own understanding or meaning related to the flow of tears. The expression of tears in the safety of the helping relationship provides the mourner with feelings of outside acceptance that results in self-compassion—and that experience is an anchor of the companion's helping role.

Misconception 5:
Being upset and openly mourning means the mourner is being "weak" in faith.

For some people it seems that having faith in God and believing in eternal life seem out of step with the open expression of grief; therefore, they repress, inhibit, or deny the expressions of thoughts and feelings related to the loss.

Be alert to those people who will teach you that they have internalized the thought that having faith and openly mourning are mutually exclusive. R. Scott Sullender noted the following related to this phenomenon: "We are accustomed to thinking that if we just had enough faith, we would not have any doubts…Some grieving people are accustomed to thinking that if they just had enough faith, they would not feel any sorrow. All of these 'accustomed' ways of thinking are unhelpful." He goes on to express that "faith is hope in a new tomorrow in spite of one's present sorrow." Yes, hope is an expectation of a good yet to be, but it doesn't mean we can detour around sorrow, pain and suffering.

The mourner may well teach you she needs gentle support as she struggles with questions of faith and grief. Encouraging and actively inviting mourners to teach you about their faith/spirituality in the context of losses usually creates sacred space to explore a variety of issues that may be part of the journey.

❖❖❖❖❖❖❖❖❖❖❖❖❖❖❖❖❖❖❖❖❖❖❖❖❖❖❖❖❖

"Faith is not a fortress. We are not locked into it. My faith has become more honest as I have grown. But it is not easy. Have faith in the searching. Loss is the platform on which we build a deeper, sturdier faith."—Rabbi David Wolpe

❖❖❖❖❖❖❖❖❖❖❖❖❖❖❖❖❖❖❖❖❖❖❖❖❖❖❖❖❖

When the timing and pacing seems right, (i.e., they give you cues that they want to explore such questions and feel safe with you to do so), encourage the mourner to teach you such things as:

• Her personal faith/spiritual history
• Does she feel comforted by her faith/spirituality?
• Are there areas of struggle related to her faith/spirituality?
• What meaning or value does she find in her religious faith, spirituality, or philosophy of life?
• What messages does she tell herself about the expression or repression of grief related to faith?
• In what ways does she find meaning in expressing her faith/ spirituality right now?

Being present to mourners as a companion means being willing to have them teach you how their faith/spirituality impacts the experience of grief. In my experience, to come along on this part of the journey is both an honor and a privilege.

Misconception 6:
When someone dies, the mourner only grieves and mourns for the physical loss of the person.

When someone dies, the mourner does not just experience the loss of the physical presence of the person. As a caregiver you have an obligation to be respectful of the multitude of ripple-effect losses that often impact the grieving person. What follows is an outline of these potential losses. Obviously this outline is not intended to be all-inclusive or mutually-exclusive.

Loss of self

• self ("I feel like part of me died when he died.")
• identity (The mourner may have to rethink roles as husband or wife, mother or father, son or daughter, best friend, etc.)
• self-confidence (Some grievers experience lowered self-esteem. Naturally, mourners may have lost one of the people in their lives who gave them confidence.)
• health (Physical symptoms of mourning)
• personality ("I just don't feel like myself...")

Loss of security

- emotional security (Emotional source of support is now gone, causing emotional upheaval.)
- physical security (Mourners may not feel as safe living in their homes as they did before.)
- fiscal security (Mourners may have financial concerns or have to learn to manage finances in ways they didn't before.)
- lifestyle (The mourner's lifestyle doesn't feel the same as it did before.)

Loss of meaning

- goals and dreams (Hopes and dreams for the future can be shattered.)
- faith (Mourners often question their faith.)
- will/desire to live (Mourners often have questions related to future meaning in their lives. They may ask, "Why go on...?")
- joy (Life's most precious emotion, happiness, is naturally compromised by the death of someone we love.)

You have the opportunity to bring active empathy to the mourner by staying sensitive and being responsive to the need to explore those various secondary losses.

Misconception 7:
The mourner should try not to think about the person who died on holidays, anniversaries, and birthdays.

This misconception is closely aligned with the misconception that it is better to move away from grief and mourning instead of toward it. The mourner often discovers that her heart and soul naturally nudge her to think about the person who died during holidays, anniversaries, birthdays and other special occasions. Obviously, these are natural times for grief to well up inside and spill over—even long after the death itself.

You will find that some mourners logically, rationally think that if they avoid thinking about the person who died on these special days, that they can avoid some of the pain of the loss. Yet, as a companion you realize that soul ache has nowhere to go if it is not released. It simply

bides its time, patiently at first,
then urgently, like a caged animal,
pacing behind the bars.

Instead of helping the mourner
deny or inhibit her grief during
these times, your role as a companion is to help her give honor
or attention to whatever feelings are instinctively trying to surface.
Many people appreciate help exploring ways to commemorate the life
of the person who died by doing something he or she would have
appreciated. You can help the mourner find creative ways to honor the
special passions of the person who died or ways to remember her life.
You can encourage mourners to spend time in the company of people
with whom they feel safe and find comfort.

*"Love is, above all, the gift
of oneself."* —Jean Anouilh

Misconception 8:
The mourner should be able to "get over" grief as
soon as possible.

If you trust in the art of companioning, you probably believe as I do
that the helping role is not about getting people "over" grief.
However, you will probably find that many mourners have been contaminated by this misconception and internalized it.

In part, your helping role related to this misconception is to free the
mourner from this linear model of understanding her experience. Of
course this is challenging if she has people around her who ask questions like, "Are you over it yet?" or, even worse, tell her she should be
"over it." Sadly, in a mourning-avoidant culture most mourners will
get some of these types of messages, either directly or indirectly.

As a companion you do help your fellow human beings integrate loss
into life and ultimately into the fabric of their beings. This entire concept is discussed more in Wisdom Teaching Five, page 181.

For now, suffice it to say that the helping role is not about getting
people over grief. Instead, it is grounded in creating safe, sacred space

for mourners to actively look and see how they are transformed and create Divine Momentum for "reconciliation," not "resolution."

Misconception 9:
Nobody can help the mourner with the grief/mourning journey.

You will find there is a group of mourners who project that no one can help them with their grief. They often have difficulty seeking and accepting support. They often carry a message they started getting in childhood along the lines of, "If you want something done right, do it yourself." Yet, in reality the most compassionate thing people can do for themselves is to reach out for help from others.

Obviously, sharing the pain of loss with others won't make it disappear, but it will over time make it more bearable. By definition, mourning (i.e., the outward expression of grief) requires that we all get some support from outside sources. Reaching out for help also connects the mourner to other people and strengthens the bonds of love that make life seem worth living. Social support is one of the most critical influences on a bereaved person's capacity to integrate loss into life.

❖❖❖❖❖❖❖❖❖❖❖❖❖❖❖

He that is thy friend indeed,
He will help thee in thy need:
If thou sorrow, he will weep;
If you wake, he cannot sleep;
Thus of every grief in heart
He with thee doth bear a part...
—Richard Barnfield

❖❖❖❖❖❖❖❖❖❖❖❖❖❖❖

Your companioning role surrounding this misconception is to help encourage an awareness of the importance of using existing support systems. Where you discover support systems do not exist you can often serve as an advocate of the need to create them. Primarily you are helping mourners realize that getting help from others is not a sign of weakness, but rather a sign of compassionate and well-deserved self-care.

Misconception 10:
When grief and mourning are finally reconciled, they never come up again.

It only makes sense that mourners hope there is some discrete endpoint to the grief journey. Yet, experience usually teaches them there is no magical day where they wake up and never ever experience feelings connected to the death of someone precious (or even the death of someone they had a difficult relationship with).

Sometimes heightened periods of sadness overwhelm the mourner—even years after the death. These times can seem to come out of nowhere and can be frightening and painful. Grief comes in and out like waves from the ocean. Sometimes when the mourner least expects it, a huge wave comes along and pulls her feet right out from under her. Sometimes something as simple as a sound, or smell or sight can bring on one of these "griefbursts."

Your companioning role is to help the mourner experience the ebbs and flows of the journey without shame or self-judgment, no matter where or when they occur. Provide some anticipatory guidance that they will probably sooner or later experience one of these "griefbursts" when they are around other people, maybe even strangers. Help them recognize that they will probably come to know whom they can share these griefbursts with and whom they cannot.

"Life is eternal, and love is immortal, and death is only a horizon; and a horizon is nothing save the limit of our sight."
— Rossiter Worthington Raymond

You can help mourners come to understand that it is normal and appropriate that, for the rest of their lives, they will feel some grief related to life losses. It will no longer dominate their lives (if they find people and places to authentically mourn), but it will always be there, in the background, reminding the mourner of the relationship they had with people who have died.

The misconceptions outlined above are certainly not all-inclusive. However, they are some of the more common misconceptions that grieving people have taught me that they have internalized. In sum, your helping role around this "wisdom teaching" is to supportively dispel these misconceptions and, in doing so, help create Divine Momentum for authentic mourning in a culture that often makes doing so a challenge.

Wisdom Teaching Two:
Consider the Influences on the Mourner's Unique Journey Into Grief

In life, out of the capacity to give and receive love comes the necessity to mourn. Yet, no two people's grief journeys are ever the same. Just as people die in different ways, people grieve and mourn in different ways.

This important wisdom teaching reminds you that as a companion, you must bear witness as mourners teach you about the unique reasons that their grief is what it is—the "whys" of their unique experience. Outlined below is an introductory overview of some of the major factors that influence a person's particular response.

While the factors are introduced, they are not intended to be all-inclusive; your awareness of them will enhance your capacity to supportively empathize with the mourner. Following each factor are questions for you as a companion to keep in mind as you enter the helping relationship.

Influence 1
The Nature of the Relationship with the Person Who Died

Different people will have their own unique response to the same loss based on the relationship that existed between the mourner and the person who died. For example, with the death of a parent, observers will note that adult children from the same family will often grieve in totally different ways. Each child's grief is based on such influences as the prior attachment in the relationship and the function the relationship served for him or her. Obviously, as a companion you supportively encourage people to teach you about the unique meaning of the loss based on the unique relationship.

Some people may teach you they need to mourn for what they wish they could have had in a relationship, but never experienced. Other people may teach you that there were strong components of ambivalence, wherein they may have loved someone yet disliked their behaviors. We often see this when someone who has struggled with chemical dependency dies. The survivors are naturally set up for struggles with their grief journey in situations like this. The key is to view the loss of the relationship from the mourner's perspective and be certain you do not make assumptions about what you think they should feel.

❖❖❖❖❖❖❖❖❖❖❖❖❖

"Lots of people want to ride with you in the limo, but what you want is someone who will take the bus with you when the limo breaks down."
—Oprah Winfrey

❖❖❖❖❖❖❖❖❖❖❖❖❖

Companioning Questions to Ask Yourself:

- What was the nature of the relationship between the grieving person and the person who died?
- What roles did the dead person play in the mourner's life?
- What was the level of attachment in the relationship?
- Were there any components of ambivalence in the relationship? If so, what was the root of the ambivalence?

Influence 2
The Circumstances of the Death

The circumstances surrounding the death have a tremendous impact on the survivor's grief journey. Among the circumstances that you as a companion need to be aware of are the age of the person who died, the suddenness of the death, and any sense of the death's perceived preventability.

The age of the person who died naturally impacts the capacity to integrate the "acceptance" of the death. To have one's aged parent die after a long-lived life is a major contrast to the death of a child whose life has only just begun. In addition, within the order of the world we anticipate that parents will die before their children. When a child dies it is an assault on the natural course of anticipated life events. Another example of the impact of age is when the 40-year-old person who is thought to be in the prime of his life dies.

Numerous studies have noted the reality that having the opportunity to anticipate a death assists in the mourner's integration of the loss into life. Sudden, unexpected loss, on the other hand, does not allow the griever any opportunity for cognitive, emotional, or spiritual preparation. In effect, the person comes to grief before she is prepared to mourn.

As companion, you will be well served to recognize that having the opportunity to anticipate a death does not lessen one's grief; however, it does provide time to do some preparation for the eventual reality of the death. Also, remember all the many mourners who have taught us, "Even when you think you are ready for the death, you really aren't." This is often the difference between thinking you are ready in your head (cognitive part of the experience) versus experiencing the reality of the death in your heart (emotional and spiritual part of the experience).

Those who have persistent thoughts that they should have been able to prevent the death naturally experience complications in the grief journey. While it is very natural for mourners to explore their own cul-

To An Athlete Dying Young

The time you won your town the race
We chaired you through the market-place;
Man and boy stood cheering by,
And home we brought you shoulder-high.
To-day, the road all runners come,
Shoulder-high we bring you home,
And set you at your threshold down,
Townsman of a stiller town.
—A.E. Houseman

pability upon the death of someone loved, some people continue to blame themselves over long periods of time.

While a sense of preventability at times evolves from the mourner's own unrealistic perceptions, you will see some people whose behavior could, in fact, have had an impact on the outcome of the death that occurred. For example, the person who makes the decisions for others that "we will all stay and ride out the hurricane" will naturally feel responsible if someone loved dies in the storm. I have also met numerous people who have fallen asleep while driving a car, resulting in an accident and the death of a passenger.

◇◇◇◇◇◇◇◇◇◇◇◇◇◇◇

"Guilt is perhaps the most painful companion of death."
—Coco Chanel

◇◇◇◇◇◇◇◇◇◇◇◇◇◇◇

The circumstance of the death can also be influenced by the mode of death, such as suicide, homicide, or AIDS. Each mode of death has special features that you as a companion are well served to familiarize yourself with so you can be empathetically responsive to the needs of the mourner.

In our mobile culture, a growing circumstance is that many people impacted by a death are separated or isolated from the location in which the death occurred. This distance results in many people having a more difficult time acknowledging the reality of the death.

Sometimes a complicator in the circumstances of the death is the lack of recovery of an identifiable body. Again, this makes it naturally difficult to believe the person has died.

Obviously there are a multitude of factors related to the circumstances of the death that shape the "why" of the mourner's response. As a companion, your role is to gently encourage and support the mourner to teach you about the unique circumstances and to bring sensitivity through empathetic responsiveness.

- What were the circumstances surrounding the death?
- What was the age of the person who died?
- What is the survivor's perception of the timeliness of the death?
- Was the death anticipated or was it sudden and unexpected?
- Does the person have a persistent sense that he should have been able to prevent the death?
- What was the mode of death? What are the special features related to the mode of death?
- Was there any separation or isolation from events surrounding the death?
- Was there an identifiable body? Was the survivor able to spend time with the body?
- What other factors might need consideration related to the unique circumstances of the death?

Influence 3
The Availability of Support Systems:
The Encouragement to Mourn from the Support System and the Mourner's Capacity to Seek and Accept Support

The very definition of mourning—the shared social response to loss—speaks to the vital importance of support systems in grief. As a companion, you will want to gently encourage the mourner to teach you about a variety of aspects that relate to support system influences.

First, you will need to learn if the mourner has support, while keeping in mind and heart that not everyone does. The lack of consistent, compassionate support systems makes for a naturally complicated mourning experience. To integrate loss into one's life requires the support of empathetic and hope-filled people. Part of your helping role is anchored in creating Divine Momentum to help activate effective support in the life of the mourner.

You will discover some mourners who appear to have support systems, yet find over time that in reality, little patience, compassion, and extended support are in the environment. Examples would include family, friends, faith communities, or other groups that may not legitimize the feelings surrounding the grief process. You will also observe that when there are stigmatized circumstances of death (e.g., suicide, homicide, AIDS), mourners are more at risk for not receiving support.

❖❖❖❖❖❖❖❖❖❖❖❖❖

The Rule of Thirds

I have discovered that, in general, you can take all the people in your life and divide them into thirds when it comes to grief support. One-third will turn out to be neutral in response to grief; they will neither help nor hinder you in your journey. One-third will turn out to be harmful to you in your efforts to mourn and heal. And one-third will turn out to be truly empathetic helpers. They will be your companions in the journey through grief.

❖❖❖❖❖❖❖❖❖❖❖❖❖

You will also find that some people have support early on in the grief journey only to have this support rapidly dwindle in the weeks, months, and years that follow. Yet, for integration of loss to occur, support must be available and made use of as the journey unfolds. North America's short social norms, borne of a too-linear understanding of grief, sometimes make getting ongoing support very difficult.

Some have support available, yet have difficulty making use of it. Some people perceive that if they accept help they are being "weak." This often traces back to their family of origin, where they were taught early in life to "do it on your own," or, "If you want something done right, do it yourself." These people may tend to over-isolate themselves and continue to demonstrate difficulty accepting others' efforts to be of help to them.

In contrast, you will encounter people who are very good at seeking and accepting support. They seem to understand the value of surrendering to the reality that the work of mourning is not something they can do by themselves. They often seek out not only individual support and group support but try to read available resources about grief and how to integrate loss into their lives. Obviously, they are open to your efforts to help them and may also be very open in expressing appreciation to you.

- Does the mourner have a support system available?
- Do the support systems they acknowledge legitimize the feelings surrounding the grief process?
- Are there any stigmatized circumstances surrounding the death that put the mourner at risk for not receiving support?
- Is support available on an extended basis?
- Is anyone projecting impatience with the mourner?
- Is the mourner willing and able to accept support?
- Do any family of origin messages around seeking and accepting support influence the mourner positively or negatively?
- How does the mourner respond to your individual effort to be supportive to her?

Influence 4
The Unique Personality of the Griever

Just as each person's personality is unique, so too is the grief response. Previous ways of being in the world and responding to other losses often are, to some extent, predictive of a person's response to the death of someone loved.

If the griever has tended to run away from crises, she may do the same thing now. If, however, she has always confronted crises head-on and openly expressed thoughts and feelings, she may do the same in this situation.

Whatever the personality of the mourner, rest assured it will be reflected in the grief experience. As noted under support system influences, those who have previously demonstrated the capacity to seek support will often seek support. In contrast, those who have demonstrated dif-

❖❖❖❖❖❖❖❖❖❖❖❖❖❖❖

"At bottom every man knows well enough that he is a unique human being, only once on this earth; and by no extraordinary chance will such a marvelously picturesque piece of diversity in unity as he is ever be put together a second time."
—Friedrich Nietzche

❖❖❖❖❖❖❖❖❖❖❖❖❖❖❖

ficulty in seeking support will often follow this same pattern of behavior now. You often see an accentuation of the person's basic personality during this time of stress.

Other personality factors, such as self-esteem, values, beliefs, and needs, also naturally influence the person's response to the death. As you companion the mourner, you are getting to know her and how she sees her world and relates to it. Be patient and she will teach you how her personality is a major influence on her response to the death.

Potential sources of complications related to the mourner's personality include but are not limited to the following:

• Prior history of struggles with depression or anxiety
• Prior history of difficulties in embracing emotions in general, particularly feelings of sadness and loss
• Prior history of distorted feelings surrounding anger, guilt, or other emotions that can be aspects of the grief experience
• Unreconciled thoughts and feelings related to prior losses in life (in other words, losses they have grieved, but not mourned)

Obviously the personality that the mourner brings into the loss experience has a tremendous impact on how grief is uniquely experienced. Therefore, as caregivers we should be very careful about generalizing about how people respond to grief and loss.

Companioning Questions to Ask Yourself:

• How has the person responded to prior losses in life?
• What was the person's personality like prior to the loss?
• How does this person's personality impact the use of support systems?
• How do factors such as self-esteem, values, beliefs, and needs appear to influence the person's response to death?
• Do you observe any potential sources of complications related to the mourner's personality? If so, what are they?
• What personality strengths will serve this person well on the grief journey?

Influence 5
The Unique Personality of the Person Who Died

Just as the mourner's unique personality is reflected in the grief experience, so too is the unique personality of the person who died. As you learn from the mourner, you will get a flavor of what the person who died was like. When I think of the flavor of the person's life, I think about this being what they brought to the "dance" of the mourner's life. A large part of what the mourner misses is often what was brought to the dance!

As a companion, use your compassionate curiosity to explore questions such as:

• What role(s) did the dead person play in the life of the mourner?
• Was the person easy to love?
• Was the person easy to live with?
• Are there things the mourner doesn't miss about the person who died?

Is there a need to mourn the lack of some things in the relationship (for example, unconditional love)? Some mourners may teach you that they wish they could have changed some aspect of the personality of the dead person, and now that he is gone, there is a final realization that that will not happen.

◇◆◇◆◇◆◇◆◇◆◇◆◇◆◇◆◇◆◇

"After (her) death I began to see her as she had really been. It was less like losing someone than discovering someone."
—Nancy Halle

◇◆◇◆◇◆◇◆◇◆◇◆◇◆◇◆◇◆◇

Mourners also may express a real need to explore ambivalence related to the person who died. While they may miss the person, there may be things about the person they don't miss. An illustration of this is when an alcohol-dependent person dies. The mourner may miss the person, but he may be relieved that he no longer has to experience some of the person's behavior. The importance of having a non-judgmental companion to express this to can be invaluable.

Sometimes the mourner will teach you that the dead person was the anchor or soothing stabilizer within the family. The person managed to "keep the family together." In the absence of the stabilizing force, the surviving family experiences a 'ripple effect" of loss in that they don't gather in the way they once did.

Most mourners find value in reviewing what the dead person brought or didn't bring to their lives. Your role is to bear witness and bring non-judgment to the power of the stories they express to you. While you cannot change what the mourner experienced because of the personality of the dead person, you can give attention to what she did experience. As a caregiver, you are affirming the mourner and helping her understand the meaning of this loss in her life.

Companioning Questions to Ask Yourself:

• What was the personality of the person who died?
• What role(s) did the dead person play in the life of the mourner?
• What does the mourner miss the most about the person who died?
• What does the mourner miss the least about the person who died?
• Is there any ambivalence related to the person who died? If so, what is that about and how is it influencing the mourner's response to the loss?
• Was the person who died an anchor or stabilizer in the mourner's life? If so, how is that reality influencing the mourner's grief journey?

Influence 6
The Ethnic/Cultural Background of the Mourner

The mourner's ethnic/cultural background is an important part of how he experiences and expresses grief. Different cultures are known for the various ways in which they express or repress their grief. As a companion you must bring sensitivity and a willingness to be taught about how responses to loss interface with the norms of each unique culture.

Culture includes the values, rules, beliefs and traditions that guide the mourner. These influences have often been handed down generation after generation and are shaped by the countries or areas of the world from which one's family originally came.

The world we live in today is really a mosaic made up of people from all types of ethnic and cultural backgrounds. As a companion you have a responsibility to bring non-judgment and an open-hearted willingness to learn about ethnic and cultural diversity and how that influences the unique experience of grief. You will also be well served to review your own background and be certain not to project your own experience onto others. For example, perhaps you come from a very emotionally expressive background yet you are companioning someone with roots in an eastern European country who might be more quiet, if not stoic, related to emotionality.

Enjoy learning from people of different backgrounds, avoid overgeneralizations about certain cultures, and be patient as you allow the individual mourner to enrich your capacity to support her unique journey into grief.

Companioning Questions to Ask Yourself:

- What is the mourner's ethnic/cultural background?
- How does this background influence the expression or repression of grief?
- What rites and rituals are meaningful to this person in the context of her ethnic/cultural background?
- How is this mourner's ethnic/cultural background similar or different than my own background?
- What special sensitivities should I keep in mind as I companion this person?
- Is there further research I need to do to better understand this mourner's ethnic/cultural background?

Influence 7
The Religious/Spiritual/Philosophical Background of the Mourner

The personal belief systems of the mourner have a tremendous impact on the grief journey. Some mourners discover that their religion, spirituality or philosophy of life is deepened, renewed, or changed as a result of the death. Many question previously held beliefs as a natural part of the work of mourning. As a companion your role is to create a "free and open space" where the mourner can teach you how her religion, spirituality, and philosophy of life may have been impacted by the death.

Some people will teach you they feel very close to God, a Higher Power, or Creator, while others may feel more distant, or even hostile. You may need to supportively bear witness while the person asks questions such as, "Why has this happened to me?" or "What is the meaning of my continued living?" The word "faith" means to believe in something for which there is no proof. For some people, faith means believing in and following a set of religious rules. For others, faith is a belief in God, a spiritual presence, or a force that is greater than we are. When the timing is appropriate, gently encourage the person to teach you how she defines faith and how her faith is influenced by the loss.

❖❖❖❖❖❖❖❖❖❖❖❖❖❖❖

*"Blessed are those who mourn,
for they will be comforted."*
—Matthew 5:4

❖❖❖❖❖❖❖❖❖❖❖❖❖❖❖

For some people, their faith community is a major source of their support system. Some faith communities have an outreach ministry in this area of caregiving and provide individual and group support. When this support is beneficial to the mourner, your companion role is to encourage her to seek and accept these helping efforts. When the mourner hopes to receive support from a faith community, but doesn't find it, she may need to express grief over the loss of anticipated support.

Some mourners may have been taught to believe that if their faith is strong enough, there is no need to mourn. For those who internalize this misconception there is a tendency to grieve internally but not to mourn externally. When this occurs, the role of the companion is to help the mourner understand that having faith does not preclude mourning. Having faith does mean having the courage to allow yourself to mourn. Some will need the gentle reminder, "Blessed are those who mourn, for they shall be comforted."

120

A central need of mourning is to "search for meaning" in one's continued living in the face of the loss. The mourner will often find herself re-evaluating her entire life and how she is living following the death of someone in her life. She will need a supportive companion who is willing to bear witness as she explores her religious, spiritual or philosophical values, questions her attitude toward life, and renews her resources for living. This process takes patience, empathy and non-judgment in your role as companion.

Companioning Questions to Ask Yourself:

- What is the mourner's religious, spiritual or philosophical background?
- How does the person describe a relationship with God, Higher Power, or Creator?
- What does "faith" mean to this person?
- Does the mourner seek and accept support from a faith community? If so, what is the experience like for her?
- Is there any internalization of the misconception held by some that having faith means one does not need to mourn? If so, how is this influencing her experience?

Influence 8
The Mourner's Gender-Role Conditioning

This relates to how males and females are taught differently about expressing their feelings. While we want to be very careful about generalizations, many men in Western cultures are encouraged to "be strong" and to restrain themselves from the expression of painful emotions, particularly feelings of sadness and loss. Some men have difficulty tolerating the helplessness that grief often brings.

"Passion and shame torment him, and rage is mingled with his grief." —Virgil

In contrast, females may teach you they have difficulty in expressing feelings of anger and some

aspects of decision-making. Again, we must remember these are generalized stereotypes and that the role of the companion isn't to change the response of the male or female, but to understand it. The capacity to mourn transcends gender. Sometimes too much is made of the differences between genders and not enough is made of the capacity to grieve and mourn.

Companioning Questions to Ask Yourself:

• How has this person been gender-role conditioned to respond to loss?
• How does this person's generational gender-role conditioning affect her grief? (This questions ties together age and gender.)
• How can you mirror back to the mourner the possible gender-role conditioning you are bearing witness to in her grief?

Influence 9
Other Crises or Stresses in the Mourner's Life

This influence is a reminder that loss rarely occurs in isolation. What else is going on in the life of the mourner? The death of someone loved may also bring the loss of financial security, the loss of one's longtime friends and perhaps the loss of one's community.

Other people in the life of the mourner may be ill or in need of help of some kind. The mourner may have young children to care for or elderly parents with special needs.

❖❖❖❖❖❖❖❖❖❖❖

"Stress is an important dragon to slay—or at least tame—in your life."
—Marilu Henner

❖❖❖❖❖❖❖❖❖❖❖

Additional stresses like these can make it naturally complicated to mourn the death loss. As a companion you must stay sensitive to additional crises or stresses and help the mourner understand how these may naturally slow down, inhibit, and complicate the grief experience.

- What other crises or stresses are influencing the life of the mourner at this time?
- How are these crises or stresses impacting the mourning experience?

Influence 10
The Mourner's Prior Experiences With Death

We now live in what has been termed "the world's first death-free generation." This means that it is now possible for a person to grow into adulthood without having experienced a close personal loss. While it is nice that people are living longer, many survivors come naked to the experience. In other words, they have had little if any preparation for coming to grief and needing to mourn. Because it is new and often frightening, the instinct for many is to want to "take flight" from it.

The role of companion is to understand this instinct while helping the mourner come to embrace the need to acknowledge the loss and authentically mourn.

"For a double grief came upon them, and a groaning for the remembrance of things past."
—Solomon Ibn Gabirol

In contrast, some mourners experience loss overload where they experience a multitude of deaths in a short amount of time. This can overwhelm the capacity to cope and demand specialized care by those trained to assist in these circumstances.

Companioning Questions to Ask Yourself:

- What is the mourner's previous experience with death loss?
- How have these previous experiences influenced their attitudes and behaviors related to grief?
- Do I have specialized knowledge and training to companion people with "loss overload"? If not, whom could I refer this mourner to for assistance?

Influence 11
The Mourner's Ritual or Funeral Experience

Decisions mourners make related to the funeral can either help or hinder the grief journey. While there is no single right way to have a funeral, we do know that creating a meaningful ritual for survivors can assist in the social, emotional, and spiritual healing after a death.

The funeral is a time and a place for mourners to express feelings about the death. The funeral also can serve as a time to honor the person who has died, bring people together for needed support, affirm that life goes on even in the face of death, and give a context of meaning that is in keeping with the mourner's own religious, spiritual, or philosophical background.

◇◇◇◇◇◇◇◇◇◇◇◇◇◇◇◇◇◇

"Believe, when you are most unhappy, that there is something for you to do in the world. So long as you can sweeten another's pain, life is not in vain." —Hellen Keller

◇◇◇◇◇◇◇◇◇◇◇◇◇◇◇◇◇◇

In many ways, the funeral is about creating Divine Momentum to help you convert your grief into mourning. A well-planned funeral helps people "know what to do" when they do not know what to do. If the primary purposes of the funeral is minimized or distorted in some way, it may well complicate the healing process for mourners.

The magical power of ceremony is that it helps people begin to heal. A meaningful funeral is really a good beginning, not, as you may have heard, "closure" or "the end." As a companion, encourage people to teach you how ceremonies have either helped or hindered their grief experience.

Companioning Questions to Ask Yourself:

• What was the mourner's experience with the funeral?
• Did the funeral experience aid in the expression or repression of her grief?

• What role does the mourner believe the funeral played in his experience with grief?

Influence 12
The Mourner's Physical Health

Grief impacts the body just as it impacts the spirit. The mourner's physical condition will influence the capacity to cope with the demands of grief.

If the mourner has a pre-existing physical illness, there will be even more vulnerability during this time. If the mourner is ill, the bodily symptoms may be as, if not more, pressing than the emotional or spiritual ones. An excellent standard of care is to encourage the mourner to get a general medical examination so that both you, the companion, and she, the mourner, have an awareness of her physical well-being.

Companioning Questions to Ask Yourself:

• Has the mourner had a recent physical examination? If so, when?
• What is the general physical condition of the mourner?
• Is the mourner currently taking any medications? If so, what?
• Who is the mourner's primary care physician?

While the above list is not all-inclusive, it will aid you in understanding the mourner's unique experience with grief. On occasions, you may find it helpful to review these influences, as well as those questions to ask yourself as a companion.

"Did you ever know, dear, how much you took away with you when you left? I was wrong to say the stump was recovering from the pain of the amputation. I was deceived because it has so many ways to hurt me that I discover them only one by one."—C.S. Lewis

Wisdom Teaching Three:
Bear Witness to the Dimensions of Grief

The previous wisdom teaching was anchored in the importance of acknowledging the uniqueness of the mourner's response and noted that neither does grief conform to a certain timeframe, nor is its expression limited to definite thoughts, feelings, and behaviors. This precludes a view of the experience of grief as one in which any specific individual will follow a definitely prescribed pattern (such as the "stages of grief").

A vital helping role of the companion is attending to those thoughts, feelings, and behaviors that may be expressed by the mourner. Then, being aware of those experiences, the companion's role is to enter into and empathetically respond in ways that assist the person in integrating the loss into a forever transformed life.

What follows is a multidimensional model of the adult grief experience. A broad outline of the model explored here is provided in the following chart. Please note that three broad classifications of grief, titled EVASION-ENCOUNTER-RECONCILIATION, are provided along with a more detailed description of components of these experiences. By no means do I pretend that this model is all-inclusive; however, I do hope it supports you in your companioning efforts.

Not every person will experience each and every response described and certainly not in the order outlined. Some regression will occur along the way and without doubt some overlapping. Unfortunately, a human being's response to loss is never as uncomplicated as described by the written word. You will note the word "dimension" of grief—as opposed to "stage" of grief—is used in an effort to

	EVASION from the new reality	ENCOUNTER with the new reality	RECONCILIATION to the new reality
Mourning characteristics	Shock Denial Numbness Disbelief	Disorganization, confusion, searching, yearning Generalized anxiety, panic, fear Physiological changes Explosive emotions Guilt, remorse, assessing culpability Loss, emptiness, sadness Relief, release	The capacity to organize and plan one's life toward the future The establishment of new and healthy relationships The capacity to being open to more change in one's life
Primary needs of mourner	Self-protection Psychological shock-absorber	Experience and expression of the reality of the death Tolerate the emotional suffering	Convert the relationship with the person who died from one of presence to one of memory Develop a new self-identity Relate the loss to a context of meaning
Time course (specific times are difficult to predict)	Weeks, potentially months (variable)	Many months, often years (variable)	No specific time-frame
Primary role of companion	Supportive presence Assist with practical matters	Encourage expression of thoughts, feelings Stabilizing, comforting presence	Supportive encouragement, hope Understanding, available presence Divine Momentum Not attached to outcome

avoid the connotation that the experience of grief occurs in some kind of orderly fashion.

The art of companioning reminds us that it is quite acceptable for mourners to be adrift rather than on some kind of "managed" course. A "hospitable" presence is about creating a free and open sacred space where the mourner can enter and become a friend. This is the dedicated presence of the companion, unhampered by judgments, no plan to fix or change the mourner or impose personal projections.

In the Buddhist tradition, Avalokiteshavara is the Buddha of compassion, whose name literally means "he who hears the cries of those in pain." A companioning presence requires listening from the heart and attending without the felt need to control or manage a fellow human being's grief. This demands an engaged focus that happens best when opening one's heart to the role of caring witness. It is certainly not about being a grief expert who claims superior knowledge of someone else's journey.

The companion bears witness without being distracted. The companion accepts thoughts and feelings without feeling a need to interpret or change thoughts and feelings. The companion experiences a genuine caring surrounding the special needs of the mourner.

We hope that the mourner who is suffering in our presence discovers that it is all right to be confused, depressed, anxious and out of control. She knows she will not be expected to "buck up" or efficiently "get on with life." She knows she will not be talked out of her pain and suffering with Bible quotes or philosophical platitudes. We hope that the mourner who is broken begins to feel safe in her psyche in this environment of unconditional love and empathy. She has discovered a companion who can be present to her in her darkness. Her brokenness can become visible as we companions "watch out for," "keep and honor" and "bear witness" to the transformative experience of grief.

Bodhichitta is a Sanskrit word meaning "noble or awakened heart." When you experience bodhichitta you allow the pain and suffering of others to touch your heart and you turn it into compassion. Instead of pushing pain away, you open your heart and allow it to touch your "well of reception."

Authentic compassion happens when you accept the mourner as an equal, all the while knowing there is nothing you can do to instantly relieve pain and suffering. While you are not responsible for curing the mourner, you are being responsible for seeking to empathize and understand what the depth of the pain and suffering feels like. Then, as you companion your fellow human being, you resonate in a helping attitude that says, "Let us sit beside one another and explore this together. Allow me to be totally present to you as we bear witness to your special needs together." This collegial attitude of compassion serves to soften and purify your heart and brings you to a sacred space of unconditional love.

In the expression of this compassionate curiosity, the companion trusts that going fully into the dark opens the mourner to the light. The paradox is that going further into the depths of suffering is what creates access to the hope of re-entering the light of a purpose-filled life. The companion does not have to rush healing or demand "resolution."

The companion stays present to what is without trying to treat ("to drag") it away or get the mourner "over it." The companion provides a container in which even the most overwhelming times of darkness can be affirmed and survived. The companion is fully present because he brings a beginner's mind and is not attached to outcome.

The companion recognizes that releasing any and all urges to fix unlocks the capacity to be present to someone in the wilderness of grief. There is an awareness that when someone is suspended in the anguish of grief, appropriate care is not trying to get him back in control, but rather sitting with him in the dark. This takes large doses of humility—and humility is about accepting reality without trying to outsmart or fix it.

Having reviewed these foundational assumptions of the role of the companion, let's familiarize ourselves with some of the more common dimensions of the grief experience and the helping role. Do remind yourself that all of these dimensions of response are shaped by the influences on grief and mourning outlined in the previous chapter.

Shock/Numbness/Denial/Disbelief

The constellation of shock, numbness, denial and disbelief is often nature's way of temporarily protecting the mourner from the reality of the death of someone loved. In reflecting on this experience, most mourners make comments like, "I was there, but yet I really wasn't," "It was like a dream," or "I managed to do what needed to be done, but I didn't feel a part of it." Reports of feeling dazed and stunned are very common during this time.

When little, if any, opportunity was available to anticipate a death, this constellation of experiences is naturally heightened. However, even when the death of someone loved is expected, we still often see components of shock, numbness, denial, and disbelief.

Shock and numbness create an insulation from the reality of the death until one is more able to tolerate what one doesn't want to believe. These emotions serve as a "temporary time out" or "psychological shock-absorber." Our emotions need time to catch up with what our minds have been told. At one level, the mourner knows the person is dead, yet is not able or willing to believe it. This distancing of the pain of the loss is instructive and helps the mourner prepare for the eventual encounter with the pain and suffering.

◇–◇–◇–◇–◇–◇–◇–◇–◇–◇–◇–◇–◇

"At other times it feels like being mildly drunk, or concussed. There is a sort of invisible blanket between the world and me. I find it hard to take in what anyone says." —C.S. Lewis

◇–◇–◇–◇–◇–◇–◇–◇–◇–◇–◇–◇–◇

Often people do not remember specific words that are spoken to them during this period of time. The mind is blocking and is not connected to listening. However, people do remember how they were made to feel by those around them. This speaks to how non-verbal presence at this time is more important than any words spoken.

This constellation of experiences acts as an anesthetic; the pain is there, but one does not experience it in its full reality. In a very real sense the body and mind take over in an effort to help the person survive. Typically a physiological component accompanies this experience, including a take-over by the autonomic nervous system. Heart palpitations, queasiness, stomach pain, and dizziness are among the most common symptoms.

A wide spectrum of what might be termed bizarre behaviors in other contexts is often observed. Hysterical crying, outbursts of anger, laughing, and fainting are frequently witnessed at this time. In actuality, expressing these behaviors allows for survival. Unfortunately, people around mourners at this time will often try to suppress these outbursts. Many of you as caregivers can probably recount experiences of being called in to "quiet the griever."

This dimension of the grief experience typically reflects only the beginning of the person's journey through grief. However, it's important to note that many people, both lay and professionals, acknowledge these experiences as being the entire mourning process. This phenomenon is reflected in the often-heard comment from the bereaved person: "People were there for me right at the time of the death and for a short time after, but they quickly returned to their routines and seemed to forget about me and my need for support and understanding." These kinds of statements tell companions something very important about not only being available at the time of the death, but for a long time thereafter.

The process of beginning to embrace the full reality of the death and move beyond this dimension of one's grief varies widely. Shock and numbness wane only at the pace one is able and ready to acknowledge feelings of loss. To provide a specific timeframe for everyone would be to over-generalize. Obviously, there is a close relationship between the circumstances of the death and the readiness to encounter the full reality of the loss.

However, even after one becomes capable of embracing the reality of the loss, sometimes this dimension still comes to the surface. This particularly is seen at such times as the anniversary of death or other special occasions (birthdays, holidays, etc.). I also have repeatedly witnessed the resurgence of this dimension when the person visits a place associated with a special memory of the dead person.

In actuality, the person's mind approaches and retreats from the reality of a death over and over again, as he tries to embrace and integrate the meaning of the death into his life. The availability of a consistent support system allows this process to occur. During this process of acknowledging one's grief, at times the hope still is that one will wake up from a bad dream and that none of this will have really happened.

The Companion's Helping Role. Critical to the helping role at this time is to acknowledge that shock, numbness, denial, and disbelief are not something to be discouraged, but instead something to be understood and allowed. To do anything else would be an attempt to take a person's grief away from her. A significant amount of the mourner's natural behavior during this dimension results in attempts to have other people care for her at a time when she is unable to do so.

In my experience, the primary task of the companion at this time is to simply "be with" the mourner. Remember, we are aware that people do not, at this time, remember specific words that are said to them, but do remember how they are made to feel by those around them. Quiet, caring, supportive companionship often becomes the person's greatest need at this time.

The art of being physically, emotionally, and spiritually present, while at the same time not invading the mourner's space, is not always an easy task. When we as helpers feel helpless, often our first inclination is to talk too much. Becoming capable of acknowledging our own feelings of helplessness at this time allows us to become more effective in our caregiving. In acknowledging our helplessness, we know that bombarding the person with words only serves to disorient him further. Remember, hospitality is anchored in creating free and open sacred space.

We also might want to do and say that which the mourner herself really needs to do and say at this time. Given time and support, the mourner finds value in doing and saying for herself and allows her the

Divine Momentum needed to encounter the loss on her own time-frame, not yours. Again, prevent yourself from taking this opportunity away from the individual. (Of course, practical help such as meal preparation is appreciated.)

Related to the previous statements is the awareness that during this time, the mourner will often demonstrate a natural difficulty with decision-making and anything that requires concentration. As an effective companion, do not collaborate with others who may be attempting to force decisions out of the person. If well-intentioned people are pushing for decisions, you can become an advocate for a waiting period. Decisions can and should be temporarily postponed until the person feels capable of participating in the decision-making process.

When at all possible, a quiet, physical environment should be provided to the grieving person at this time. When in shock, people become more disoriented if they are bombarded with outside noise. In a strange way, quietness becomes comforting. Providing a blanket for warmth and a hot drink are also helpful to many people at this time.

Use the person's reaction to you as a guide for your own behavior. Be careful not to project your own needs into the situation. I once heard it said that perhaps the most effective helping role at this time is: "Mouth closed, ears open, and presence available." Perhaps keeping this in mind as an underlying theme will assist you as you reach out to comfort at this most difficult time.

Disorganization/Confusion/Searching/Yearning

Perhaps the most isolating and frightening part of the grief experience is the sense of disorganization, confusion, searching and yearning that often comes with the loss. This is frequently when the mourner begins to be confronted with the reality of the death. As one woman expressed, "I felt as if I was a lonely traveler with no companion, and worse yet, no destination. It was as if I couldn't find myself or anybody else."

This is when many people experience the "going crazy syndrome." Because normal thoughts and behaviors in grief are so different from what one normally experiences, the grieving person does not know whether her new thoughts and behaviors are normal or abnormal. Those experiences described in the next paragraph are so common after the death of someone loved that they must be acknowledged as part of the normal process of mourning. A major task of the companion is to assist in normalizing, but not minimizing, these experiences.

Often present is a sense of restlessness, agitation, impatience, and ongoing confusion. An analogy that seems to fit is that it is like being in the middle of a wild, rushing river, where you can't get a grasp on anything. Disconnected thoughts race through the mourner's mind and strong emotions at times are overwhelming.

Disorganization and confusion often express themselves as an inability to complete any task. A project may get started but go unfinished. Time is distorted and seen as something to be endured. Certain times of day, often early morning and late night, are times when the person feels most disoriented and confused. Disorganization and confusion are often accompanied by fatigue and lack of initiative, what I often call "the lethargy of grief." The acute pain of the loss is devastating to the point that normal pleasures do not seem to matter.

"It doesn't seem worth starting anything. I can't settle down." —C.S. Lewis

A restless searching for the person who died is a common part of the experience. Yearning for the dead person and being preoccupied with memories of him may lead to intense moments of distress. Often a shift in perception makes other people look like the dead person. A phenomenon sometimes exists whereby sounds are interpreted as signals that the person has returned, such as hearing the garage door open and the person entering the house as she had done for so many years.

Visual hallucinations occur so frequently that they cannot be considered abnormal. I personally prefer the term "memory picture" to visual hallucination. Seemingly, as part of the searching and yearning process, the mourner not only experiences a sense of the dead person's presence, but may have transient experiences of looking across the room and seeing the person.

Other common features during this time are difficulties with eating and sleeping. Many people experience a loss of appetite while others overeat. Those people who do eat often note a lack of being able to taste their food. Difficulty in going to sleep and early morning awakening also are common experiences.

❖❖❖❖❖❖❖❖❖❖❖❖❖❖

"My heart and body are crying out, come back, come back."
—C.S. Lewis

❖❖❖❖❖❖❖❖❖❖❖❖❖❖

Dreams about the dead person are often a part of the experience at this time. Dreams are often an unconscious means of searching for the person who has died. It is often described to me by people as an opportunity to be close to the person. As one widower related, "I don't seem to have any control over it, but each night I find myself dreaming about my wife. I see us together, happy and content. If it only could be that way again." The content of these dreams often reflects the real life changes in the person's experience with mourning.

The Companion's Helping Role. During this complex dimension of grief, the mourner tends to worry about the normalcy of the experience. Thus, the mourner is not only faced with the pain of the grief, but also the fear that he may be "going crazy." Reassurance and education abut the normalcy of the experience allows the person to share thoughts, feelings, and behaviors outside of himself.

As I've noted, grief must be shared outside of oneself for healing to occur. The companion must be patient and attentive as the person tells the story over and over. Repetition occurs with what the person shares with you as she works to internalize and reconcile herself to the death that has occurred.

During this time, the mourner will sense your genuine interest in listening and attempting to understand. The person will not share her

The Awesome Power of "Telling The Story"

As my father lay in his hospital bed recovering from cancer surgery, it was my privilege to honor his life story. My wonderful father recognized in his head and heart that his days on this earth were limited. Rest did not come easy, but his need to "story" did.

His love of family flowed out of stories from his childhood. He told me how his mother inspired his love for baseball. He told me how his father wasn't very emotionally or physically available to him as he grew from childhood to adolescence. He told me of his deep love for his older brothers and sisters.

In the midst of my awareness that I would soon not have my father in my life, I listened and I learned. I affirmed that his love for me was true and abiding. I learned of his fears about my mother, who will survive him. I learned what I already knew—my father is a great man, a loving husband and a wonderful father.

I also learned about the awesome power of "telling the story." As he shifted from topic to topic, he didn't need me to get in the way. As he at times struggled with a specific detail of a long-ago memory, he didn't need me to get in the way. As he was brought to tears by his love-filled memories of life and living, he didn't need me to get in the way.

As I reflect on my all-night vigil of honoring his story, I'm once again humbled by the remarkable importance of how "storying" brings meaning and purpose to our life and death experiences. As a grief companion, I commit much of my life's vocation to honoring stories. Stories of love and loss. Stories of pain and joy. Stories of hopes fulfilled and dreams lost.

Yet, in our fast-paced, efficiency-based culture, which lacks an understanding of the role of hurt in healing, many people do not understand the value of "telling the story." Honoring stories would require that we slow down, turn inward and embrace our own and others' pain. Listening to stories filled with sadness and grief are intolerable in a culture that collectively avoids these emotions whenever possible.

Thanks Dad for reminding me not only of your love for me and our family, but of how all of us need to stop—to listen—and to honor stories about life and death. Thanks for making me proud to be a grief counselor and companion to my fellow human beings. But most of all, thanks for making me proud to be your son.

grief with you if she does not feel an open willingness to listen and understand being generated from you.

The means to move from disorganization toward reconciliation is through the expression of thoughts and feelings. The person may need to talk and cry for long periods of time. The role of the helper is not to interrupt with reasoning, but to use the companioning principles outlined in Part One of this book.

The thoughts, feelings, and behaviors of this dimension do not come all at once and are often experienced in a wave-like fashion. The mourner needs to be supported through each wave and reassured that the surges do not mean regression but are a normal part of the experience of grief. At times, the content of what the person might be saying can make little sense; however, this can be helpful and clarifying for the mourner.

During this time, the mourner should be actively discouraged from making critical decisions like selling a home and moving to another community. With the judgment-making difficulties that naturally come with this part of the experience, ill-timed decisions can often result in secondary losses.

Anxiety/Panic/Fear

Feelings of anxiety, panic, and fear are often experienced by the mourner. These feelings are typically generated from thoughts such as: "Will my life have any purpose without this person? I don't think I can live without him." The death of someone loved naturally threatens one's feelings of security and results in the evolution of anxiety.

❖❖❖❖❖❖❖❖❖❖❖❖❖

"No one ever told me that grief felt so like fear." —C.S. Lewis

❖❖❖❖❖❖❖❖❖❖❖❖❖

As the person's mind is continually brought back to the pain of loss, panic may set in. Anxiety and fear often stem from thoughts about "going crazy." The thought of being abnormal creates even more intense fear.

Fear of what the future holds; fear that one person's death will result in others; increased awareness of one's own mortality; feelings of vulnerability about being able to survive without the person; inability to concentrate; and emotional and physical fatigue all serve to heighten anxiety, panic, and fear. The mourner often feels overwhelmed by everyday problems and concerns. To make matters worse, a change may occur in economic status, large bills may need to be paid, and the fear often increases of becoming dependent on others.

The Companion's Helping Role. The major helping principle to keep in mind regarding anxiety, panic and fear is the need to explore supportively and to acknowledge these experiences within the mourner.

Not talking about fears only causes them to grow larger. Often a helpful approach is to communicate your willingness to discuss fears by providing an open-ended question such as, "People have taught me that with the death of someone loved, there are often fears that arise. Have you had any fears?" Then, follow the person's lead as they begin to explore those fears.

Support the naturalness of those fears and express your willingness to be a sounding-board for their expression. Your awareness of the common fears outlined in this section will assist you in anticipating some of what might be shared. Again, use the principles of companioning outlined in Part One of this book.

Physiological Changes

A person's body responds to what the mind has been told at a time of acute grief. Some of the most common physiological changes that the mourner may experience are as follows:

• Generalized lack of energy and fatigue
• Shortness of breath

- Feelings of emptiness in the stomach
- Tightness in the throat and chest
- Sensitivity to noise
- Heart palpitations
- Queasiness
- Difficulty in sleeping or, on other occasions, prolonged sleeping
- Headaches
- Agitation and generalized tension

With loss, the mourner's immune system breaks down and he becomes more vulnerable to illness. Many studies have documented significant increases in illness during bereavement.

In the majority of instances, physical symptoms are normal and temporary. At times, the mourner will unconsciously assume a "sick role" in an effort to legitimize his feelings to others. This often results in frequent visits to the physician. Unfortunately, assumption of the sick role often occurs when the person does not receive encouragement to mourn, or doesn't give himself permission to express thoughts and feelings in other ways.

The Companion's Helping Role. When little or no outlet exists to express feelings in a natural way, the person expresses feelings through her physical being. As a caregiver you also should be aware that physical disorders present prior to the loss tend to become worse. In addition, often what occurs is a transient identification with the physical symptoms that have caused the death of the person loved. For example, if the spouse dies of a heart attack, the mourner may complain of chest pains.

Depending on the extent of the symptoms, suggesting that the person consult a physician is appropriate to rule out physical causes for the symptoms. Every person who is seen at the Center for Loss and Life Transition is referred for a general medical examination. Helping the person understand physical symptoms as a normal facet of grief often allows these symptoms to soften as authentic mourning unfolds.

Explosive Emotions

Because of society's attitude toward anger, this dimension is often the most upsetting to those around the griever. Often, both the mourner and those trying to be supportive to the mourner have problems acknowledging and creating an environment for the expression of this wide spectrum of emotions. The reason for this is frequently related to the uncertainty of how to respond to the griever at this time.

When we think of explosive emotions, we sometimes oversimplify by talking only about anger. Yet the mourner also may experience feelings of hate, blame, terror, resentment, rage, and jealousy. While these emotions all have their distinctive features, adequate similarities exist in the person's underlying needs to warrant discussing the various explosive emotions together. Beneath the explosive emotions are the griever's more primary feelings of pain, helplessness, frustration, fear, and hurt.

Expression of explosive emotions often relates to a desire to restore things to the way they were before the death. Even though a conscious awareness is present that the person has died, the need to express explosive emotions and a desire to "get the person back" seems to be grounded in psycho-biological roots.

So while the expression of explosive emotions does not create the desired result of bringing the dead back to life, we can begin to understand why explosive emotions in grief are so common. If viewed in this fashion, anger and other related emotions can be seen as an intelligent response that the grieving person is making in an attempt to

❖◦❖

"Who still thinks there is some device (if only he could find it) which will make pain not be pain. It doesn't really matter whether you grip the arms of the dentist chair or you let your hands lie in your lap. The drill drills on."
—C.S. Lewis

❖◦❖

restore the relationship that has been lost. Actually, in my experience, there is a healthy survival value in being able to temporarily protest the painful reality of the loss. It's as if having the capacity to express anger gives one the courage to survive at this particular point in time. The griever who either doesn't give herself the permission to experience explosive emotions or doesn't receive permission from others may slide into a chronic depressive response that includes no desire to go on living.

The fact that the dead person does not come back despite the griever's explosive emotions is part of the reality-testing needed for the eventual process of reconciliation. With the gradual awareness that the person who has died will not, in fact, return, the need for the expression of these emotions changes over time. Only when the reality that the loss is permanent creeps in does the person free himself from this dimension of mourning. Should the explosive emotions become chronic, not changing over time, this would be an indication of a complicated grief response.

Let's look at some of the ways these emotions are expressed:

• Explosive emotions basically have two avenues for expression: outward or inward. What the griever does with these emotions can have a powerful impact on the journey through the grief. The anger may be expressed outwardly, toward friends and family, doctors, God, the person who died, the counselor, people who have not experienced loss, or any number of other persons or places.
• Some mourners perceive death to be a form of punishment and naturally respond with anger toward those they feel are responsible for the death. God, seen as having power over life and death, becomes a target for the expression of explosive emotion. For example, a man remarked: "I stopped attending church after my wife's death. She and I had been so devoted in our faith and yet He took her from me. I don't see any point in being faithful to Him if He is not going to be faithful to me."
• Many caregivers have taught me that they often feel the most helpless in the face of mourners expressing anger toward God. At times, the sense of a need to defend God is felt. And yet, God, in his natural "whipping post" position, probably doesn't need anyone to defend Him. As we all realize, He has been taking pretty good care

of Himself for some time now. I also would mention that having anger at God speaks of having a relationship with God. If no relationship exists, the person would probably not feel anger.

My experience suggests that as soon as you begin to defend God, you may dig yourself a hole that is difficult to get out of. Frequently the more you defend your position that the person should not be angry at God, the more the person strives to convince you that he should; your response causes the person to defend his response.

Anger toward God is not something to be judged, but instead, is something to be understood in the context of the mourner's experience. If you are able to fight any felt sense of need to defend God, you can often enter into a dialogue with the

"Why is He so present a commander in our time of prosperity and so very absent a help in time of trouble?"
—C.S. Lewis

person that allows him to search for meaning. The mourner already feels abandoned by God; certainly he doesn't need to be abandoned by you in the role of supportive companion.

In some instances, mourners will direct their anger inward, resulting in low self-esteem, depression, chronic feelings of guilt, physical complaints, and potentially suicidal thoughts. When anger is repressed and directed inward, the person's experience with grief often becomes complicated and chronic. Anger turned inward may result in agitation, tension, and general restlessness. It is as if something is inside the person trying to get out.

The Companion's Helping Role. Not all mourners experience the same depth of explosive emotions. However, many mourners will be able to relate to some of the experiences outlined in the preceding paragraphs. Therefore, in your helping role you will want to confirm these emotions when expressed and use the companioning principles outlined in Part One of this book.

A word of caution: obviously you do not want to prescribe these feelings but be alert for them. The majority of studies on mourning have focused on premature and unexpected deaths where explosive emotions are very commonly seen. However, in some situations, especially those in which a death is more anticipated, explosive emotions may be mild or not exist at all.

Ultimately, healthy grief requires that explosive emotions, when present, be expressed, not repressed. Many grieving people need a supportive listener who can tolerate, encourage, and validate explosive emotions without judging, retaliating, or arguing. The comforting presence of a caring companion often allows the person to express pent-up emotions.

Keep in mind that as a member of the helping profession, you may well be rebuffed by those very persons you would like to help. Anger can be directed toward people who attempt to comfort, because for the mourner, accepting comfort is to acknowledge the pain of the loss that has occurred.

Hostility directed toward helpers is certainly understandable. For example, if we as helpers are aware that one of the needs of mourning is to acknowledge the reality of the loss, we naturally want to assist the person in gently confronting this reality. However, at certain points in grief for some people, they are not seeking confrontation with reality, they are seeking reunion with the person who has died. So, the helper who does not take sides in the mourner's struggle between striving for reunion and acknowledging the painful reality of the loss proves to be very helpful. This is a delicate helping task whereby you are not encouraging denial, but communicating an understanding of the search for reunion. The helper who does not achieve this balance is often met with angry feelings on the part of the mourner.

For the mourner who expresses explosive emotions toward the person who died, it is important to help the mourner achieve balance between both negative and positive feelings. I have seen a number of people in counseling who will become rigidly focused on negative feelings toward the deceased as a means of preventing themselves from acknowledging the hurt, pain, and sadness associated with the loss.

Assisting the person to achieve the appropriate balance relates to the art of helping.

As you strive to help mourners in this dimension of grief, keep in mind the underlying feelings of pain, helplessness, frustration, fear, and hurt. The companion needs to be in touch with these primary feelings, and at the same time listen permissively and accept all other feelings. Through permissive listening and responsive support, the griever learns that her feelings are neither good nor bad, but are merely hers and are present. A real need at this point is for the helper to be accepting of all feelings and to support the griever as such strong and strange feelings change over time.

So, we have reminded ourselves that anger and other explosive emotions in grief can be natural and healthy. While anger will at times express itself in irrational ways, friends, family, and helpers who fail to realize this can leave the griever feeling abandoned, guilty, and confused about experiencing anger.

In reality, explosive emotions cannot and should not be prevented from being expressed. The difficulty is not the presence of these emotions, but finding and giving oneself permission to be angry. When faced with explosive emotions, the mourner is most in need of stabilizing, sustaining relationships. As a companion, you have the opportunity and privilege of creating just such a relationship.

Guilt/Remorse/Assessing Culpability

Guilt and self-blame are sometimes seen in the grieving person. A natural process of assessing one's culpability seems to occur following loss through death. Some people become obsessed by guilt, leading to a complicated grief response and the need for specialized help, while others come to understand the normalcy of temporary feelings of regret or guilt.

Guilt evolves in a number of ways as a part of the experience of grief. Perhaps the most common is the "If only I would have…" or "Why didn't I…" syndrome. This often relates to a sense of wanting to change the circumstances surrounding the death or unfinished business in the relationship with the person who died.

Some examples of common "if onlys" that you may hear the person express are:

• "If only I had known he was dying..."
• "If only I would have gotten her to the doctor sooner..."
• "If only I insisted she take better care of herself..."
• "If only I had been a better wife..."

These are only a few of the hundreds of examples that could be given. While the expression of guilt is often not logical, it is still a natural part of the healing process. Unfortunately, as helpers, we often find ourselves wanting to rush in and try to take the person's need to express guilt or self-blame away. We will explore this more in our discussion of the helper's role.

Feelings of guilt are often expressed about those days or weeks just prior to the death. Assessing one's culpability during this time often seems to be an indirect means of assuring oneself that one did everything that could have been done for the person. This is most certainly an understandable need on the part of the survivor. A common theme I often witness at this time is a desire to have created opportunities to talk with the person about her dying. For example, "If only we could have been honest with each other about what was happening."

Surviving a person who has died often generates feelings of guilt. Survival guilt leads the person to ask, "How is it that she died and I survived?" I recently saw a middle-aged man in counseling who had been driving an automobile in which his wife was a passenger. He fell asleep at the wheel and an accident occurred. His wife died instantly and he walked away without a scratch. He needed to be able to explore the question of his survival in the face of her death. In his mind, his sense of responsibility for falling asleep demanded his death, but certainly not his wife's.

Another type of guilt evolves when a person's death brings some sense of relief or release. This often occurs when the person who died had been ill for a prolonged period of time or the relationship was conflicted. In the case of a long illness, the mourner may not miss the frequent trips to the hospital or the physical responsibilities of caring for the person. If the person is not able to acknowledge this sense of relief as natural, and not equal to a lack of love, he may feel guilty for feeling relieved.

An example of the relief-guilt syndrome in a conflicted relationship is as follows: I have worked with a number of families who have experienced the death of an alcoholic member of the family. Upon the alcoholic's death, his family members often feel a sense of relief (among other emotions, of course). Again, if the survivors are able to be understanding of their sense of relief, all is well and good. However, they often get caught in the trap of the relief-guilt syndrome.

❖❖❖❖❖❖❖❖❖❖❖❖❖❖

"Still, there's no denying that in some sense I 'feel better,' and with that comes at once a sort of shame, and a feeling that one is under a sort of obligation to cherish and foment and prolong one's unhappiness." —C.S. Lewis

❖❖❖❖❖❖❖❖❖❖❖❖❖❖

Another form of guilt is that which evolves from longstanding personality factors of the survivor. Some people are taught early in life, typically during childhood, that they are responsible when anything bad or unfortunate occurs. When a death occurs in their lives, the first place they look to find blame is at themselves. Obviously, this kind of guilt relates to longstanding personality factors that merit their own work in the context of the companioning relationship.

Guilt also can be experienced when the mourner begins to re-experience any kind of joy or happiness in his life. This often is related to loyalty to the person who died and fears that being happy in some way betrays the relationship that once was. Opportunities to explore these feelings are often necessary as the person moves forward in the experience of the grief.

We often witness feelings of guilt when the survivor was not able to be present when the death occurred. Often the irrational, yet understandable, thought is, "If I had been there, the person would not have died." This often relates to a desire to have power or control over something that one has no power or control over. After all, if I feel guilty, it means I could have done something to change the outcome of what happened. This thinking seems to be an attempt to counter feelings of helplessness and impotence, which are certainly an understandable response in the context of the painful reality of the loss.

You also will witness occasions when feelings of guilt will be induced by those around the griever. This often occurs through ignorance, lack of understanding, or the need to project outside of oneself onto others. Projecting outside of oneself is illustrated by family members who, wanting to deny their own pain and any sense of culpability, lash out at other family members.

An unfortunate example of guilt induction is the family friend who informs the recently bereaved widow, "Your husband would not have died if you had had a closer relationship with God." These kinds of messages often become very destructive to the mourner who is already struggling with grief.

People sometimes feel guilty for having had a conscious or unconscious wish for the death of someone who did in fact die. We call this magical thinking, which is the notion that somehow one's thoughts can cause action. The majority of relationships have components of ambivalence wherein a person will think, on occasion, "I wish you would go away and leave me alone." In some highly conflicted relationships, people have even more direct thoughts of wanting the relationship to end. When the person does die, the survivor may have a sense that he somehow caused the death.

While all relationships have periods of time when negative thoughts are experienced, obviously one's mind does not have the power to inflict death on someone. Again, however, you can easily see how the person might connect thoughts with events that occur.

Feelings of guilt are not limited to any select group of people. They are a natural part of the experience of grief. Being aware of the normalcy of guilt and the need to assess culpability should allow you to enter the helping relationship with an open mind, generous heart, and available presence.

The Companion's Helping Role. In relation to this dimension of grief, one of the companion's primary roles is that of permissive, patient, and non-judgmental listener. This allows the mourner the opportunity to explore feelings of regret or guilt and opens awareness for rebuilding.

Try to avoid the natural urge to quickly and prematurely explain the person's guilt away. Doing so won't work and we simply cannot do for the person what she must do for herself. However, you can provide a stabilizing presence that allows the mourner to assess culpability. Only in exploring what she should or should not feel guilty about does the mourner come to some understanding of what the limits of her responsibility are.

Provide opportunities for the mourner to talk about the circumstances surrounding the death. You then can do some reality-testing with the person. For example, if the mourner says, "I think I should have been of more help to him during his long illness," you might respond with, "Help me understand what you did to be of help." The mourner will then go on to relate what he did do to be of help to the person. Again, you are not judging whether he should have done more or less, but assisting him in coming to his own conclusions.

Of course, legitimate guilt can occur in situations where survivors can identify things they truly could have done differently in the relation-ship with the person who died. The art of helping this person becomes more difficult. As helpers, we all tend to have our own unique ways of working to assist people with legitimate guilt. Our reli-gious, spiritual, and philosophical backgrounds play a part in what we see as both helpful and appropriate. I can only share with you what I tend to do under these circumstances, realizing that what you do may be very different, yet equally effective.

Typically, I attempt to work within the mourner's own frame of refer-ence. I find that many people from religious backgrounds find value in confession to God and asking for forgiveness. While this doesn't fit for everyone, it does seem to fit many.

The process may go something like this: The person teaches me about his religious beliefs and I sense the mourner's need to ask for forgiveness. This leads to a discussion of the process of atonement (theologically, the word for taking care of guilt). I ask what is felt as being needed to be done related to atonement. The person tells me and we then map out a plan within the individual's frame of reference to seek atonement.

For example, a man in his 60s once shared with me that he had previously physically abused his wife who, years later, died of cancer. He was of Catholic faith and taught me about his need to be forgiven from his theological perspective. The decision was made that he would ask for God's forgiveness and confess his admitted wrongdoing to his priest. This began a process for him of: 1) seeking God's forgiveness; 2) acknowledging to himself and others what he had done wrong; 3) accepting that what had happened had happened,; 4) allowing himself to forgive himself in the eyes of his God; and 5) creating an environment for him in which to more fully mourn his wife's death. Through exploration of his guilt, this man was able to restore a lost relationship with God, and with himself. Obviously, this is only one example and helping people with guilt is often as unique as the person and the surrounding circumstances.

As a companion you also will want to be alert to the mourner's conscious need to punish herself secondary to feelings of guilt. Self-punishment is illustrated through chronic physical complaints, chronic depression, inappropriate risk-taking, self-defeating relationship choices, and general neglect of one's own well-being. These are signs and symptoms of complicated grief that require referral for specialized help.

We must acknowledge that guilt can, and often is, a component of complicated grief, particularly chronic depression, and cannot be ignored. Guilt is one of the most frequent emotional realms in which people become trapped and have difficulties. One of the worst things the mourner can do is ignore and repress feelings of guilt because of the many emotional and physical problems that likely will evolve when this occurs.

Should you note themes of unresolved and persistent guilt, you should probably consider consultation with another caregiver or someone who specializes in bereavement counseling. Depressive and self-destructive guilt can become dangerous when it goes unattended.

Loss/Emptiness/Sadness

With good reason, this constellation of feelings and experiences is often the most difficult for the griever. The full sense of loss never occurs all at once. Weeks and, more often, months pass after the death before the mourner is confronted by how much his life is changed by the loss. A person who has been a vital part of his life is no longer present. The mourner certainly has the right to have feelings of loss, emptiness, and sadness. Unfortunately, many people surrounding the mourner frequently try to take these feelings away. Friends, family, and sometimes even professional caregivers erroneously believe that their job is to distract the mourner from these feelings.

At times the grieving person has intense feelings of loss and loneliness. When these experiences initially occur, the mourner is usually very frightened. Thinking and hoping that he has already experienced the most devastating of emotions, he is usually unprepared for the depth of this experience.

◇◇◇◇◇◇◇◇◇◇◇◇◇

"The act of living is different all through. Her absence is like the sky, spread all over everything."
—C.S. Lewis

◇◇◇◇◇◇◇◇◇◇◇◇◇

Given the opportunity, the majority of mourners will share that the following times are among the most difficult: weekends, holidays; upon initially waking in the morning; late at night, particularly at bedtime; family mealtimes; upon arriving home to an empty house; and any kind of anniversary occasion. These difficult times usually have some special connection to the person who died.

Normal Grief	Clinical Depression
Responds to comfort and support	Does not accept support
Often openly angry	Irritable and may complain but does not directly express anger
Relates depressed feelings to loss experienced	Does not relate depressed feelings to a particular life event
Can still experience moments of enjoyment in life	Exhibits an all-pervading sense of doom
Exhibits feelings of sadness and emptiness	Projects a sense of hopelessness and chronic emptiness
May have transient physical complaints	Has chronic physical complaints
Expresses guilt over some specific aspect of the loss	Has generalized feelings of guilt
Has temporary impact on self-esteem	Presents a deep loss of self-esteem

Loss, emptiness, and sadness may be intense enough to be considered depression. Much debate is in the literature on grief concerning the distinction between grief and depression. Grief is accompanied by many symptoms of depression such as: sleep disturbance; appetite disturbance; decreased energy; withdrawal; guilt; dependency; lack of concentration; and a sense of losing control. Changes in one's normal capacity to function—along with these and other depressive symptoms—often results in the griever feeling isolated, helpless, and childlike. This normal regression that accompanies grief naturally impacts one's sense of esteem and well-being. The person often needs help understanding that these characteristics of mourning are temporary and will change over time.

An important responsibility is to note some differences between the normal depressive experience of grief and clinical depression. Recognizing that other caregivers may use other criteria, the following are some of the distinctions I find helpful to distinguish between depressive grief and other forms of depression.

In normal grief, the mourner responds to comfort and support, whereas depressives often do not accept support. The bereaved are often openly angry, whereas the depressive complains and is irritable but does not directly express anger. Bereaved persons can relate their depressed features to the loss they have experienced, whereas depressives often do not relate their experience to any life event. In normal grief, people can still experience moments of enjoyment in life, whereas with depressives an all-pervading sense of doom exists. Those around the griever can sense feelings of sadness and emptiness, whereas depressives project a sense of hopelessness and chronic emptiness. The griever is more likely to have transient physical complaints, whereas the depressive has chronic physical complaints. The griever often expresses guilt over some specific aspect of the loss, whereas the depressive often has generalized feelings of guilt. While the self-esteem of the griever is temporarily impacted upon, it is not the depth of loss of esteem usually observed in the depressive.

Obviously, it is not always easy to distinguish between the depression of grief and clinical forms of depressive illness. If you should find yourself in doubt regarding a differential diagnosis between the two, a wise procedure is to consult with other trained professionals. On those occasions where loss precipitates a major depressive illness, specialized medical intervention may be required, e.g., antidepressant medication.

Related to depressive features, we should note that many mourners do have transient thoughts of suicide. They often have hopes of being reunited with the person who died and think that this will allow them to escape the pain of the grief. While transient suicidal thoughts are normal and common, suicidal thoughts should always be assessed with utmost care.

Feelings of deprivation and impoverishment also are common during mourning. The mourner might long to be held and comforted, and simply wish to have the person who died to talk to. The thought often is that the one person who understood him is gone and the mourner might feel abandoned. Well-known author C.S. Lewis expressed his sense of deprivation following the death of his wife when he wrote, "Thought after thought, feeling after feeling, action after action had H. for their object. Now their target is gone. I keep on, through habit, fitting an arrow to the string, then I remember and have to lay the bow down."

The mourner who is not in an environment conducive to acknowledging and exploring experiences of intense loss, emptiness, and sadness will sometimes be in the position of being in conflict about expressing these feelings. Suppressed feelings often push for release, while the person is either discouraged by others, oneself, or both, to repress them. The frequent result is an increased sense of isolation, loss, and sadness.

The Companion's Helping Role. The frequent and regular presence of a stabilizing person is critical during this time. Because this dimension of grief is so isolating, the opportunity to communicate one's feelings to an accepting and understanding person is one means of reconnecting with the world outside of oneself. One goal of helping is to keep the mourner from feeling totally isolated and abandoned during this difficult time. Many people respond to an outreach approach, as the sense of isolation may prevent them from directly asking for support and guidance.

As a companion you need to be sensitive to indirect cues and signals that relate to this dimension of grief. The majority of grieving people do not directly bring up their need to talk about feelings of loss, emptiness, and sadness. However, indirect cues are given and when they go unheard, are misunderstood, or their urgency missed, the result is often another experience of loss for the person.

To counteract society's tendency to discourage the expression of these feelings, the griever needs to be encouraged to share thoughts and express tears. Feelings of loss, emptiness, sadness, and even depression in the face of the death of loved ones do not mean incompetence or weakness, and mourners should be helped to understand that they should not be ashamed of their feelings.

Avoid pushing for disclosure of painful feelings of loss until the mourner gives you cues of being at a point where those feelings can be shared with you. The person must feel a sense of respect from you as a helper prior to exploring painful feelings with you. The capacity to empathize with the depth of loss and sadness a person feels is often communicated through your nonverbal presence and when well-established, the person will more openly begin to share innermost thoughts and feelings with you.

Another means of helping is to assist people in understanding the value in the temporary feelings of depression that come with grief. In a sense, this depression is nature's way of allowing for a time-out while one works to heal the wounds of grief. Depression slows down the physiological system and prevents major organ systems from being damaged. These symptoms are a common part of "soul work," which precedes "spirit work."

Loss, emptiness, and sadness are part of acknowledging the reality of one's loss, and experiencing them allows valuable time to begin re-ordering one's life. Depression that comes with grief can ultimately be used to move ahead, to assess old ways of being, and to make plans for the future. Only in allowing depression to slow oneself down do these opportunities present themselves. This process of reframing the person's depression as a positive part of grief allows them to better tolerate these natural feelings.

Relief/Release

Death can bring relief and release from suffering, particularly when the illness has been long and debilitating. Many people inhibit this normal dimension of their grief, fearing that others will think they are wrong or cruel to feel this way. So, while very natural, feelings of relief and release are often difficult for the griever to talk about and admit openly.

Relief does not equal a lack of feeling for the person who died, but instead relates to the griever's response to an end to painful suffering. In addition, to feel relief is natural because death frees one of certain demands and opens up new opportunities and experiences.

I saw a 40-year-old man in counseling following the death of his 38-year-old wife. His wife had been suffering with bone cancer for the past two years. Upon her death, he was able to acknowledge his relief that she was finally free of her pain. However, he also was able, with time, to acknowledge that their marital relationship of 16 years had always been conflicted and unsatisfactory to him. He expressed release from their constant fights and his perception of their mutual chronic unhappiness in the relationship.

Feelings of relief and release also relate to the reality that we do not just begin to grieve at the moment of someone's death. The experience of grief begins when the person with whom we have a relationship enters the transition from being alive and living to dying.

When the dying process is prolonged and filled with physical and emotional pain for those involved, one might observe that family members experience some of the following anticipatory grief thoughts over time. The family's initial reaction, "he is sick, " moves toward "he is very sick" then later toward "he may die." Eventually the family begins to understand that "he is going to die" and sees "he is suffering so much." The suffering gives rise to their feeling that "we'll be glad when he is out of his pain." "He is dead" is often the next realization, which translates into natural relief: "We're relieved he is dead and out of his pain."

Death also can be experienced as relief when the apparent alternative is a continual debilitating journey with an unconscious, vegetative form of existence, chronic alcoholism, and other forms of living with little quality of life. Regardless of how loving and caring a family may be, at times chronic illness exhausts and drains everyone. When death finally comes, relief is experienced not in isolation, but amongst a number of other emotions as well.

Another aspect of relief for some people is a sense of having been spared because someone else, not they themselves, died. Again, this sense of relief is natural and some people will express a need to explore these feelings with you.

Crying and expressing the thoughts and feelings related to a loss also can be experienced as relief. I often witness a tremendous sense of relief from those who have repressed and avoided the outward expression of their grief. Being able to acknowledge the pain of their experience frequently relieves internal pressure and allows them to make movement in the journey through their grief. To the mourner, a sense of relief can occur by finding someone who is able to communicate back an empathetic understanding of her experience.

The relief that comes from acknowledging the pain of grief becomes a critical step toward reconciliation. As the pain is explored, acknowledged, and accepted as a vital part of healing, a renewed sense of meaning and purpose follows. Working to embrace relief as one of many normal feelings creates the opportunity to find hope beyond one's acute grief.

The Companion's Helping Role. The primary role of the companion is to allow for the expression of relief and communicate an understanding of its naturalness. Listen acceptingly to the griever's sense of relief without implying or increasing any feelings of shame or guilt.

As previously noted, many people do feel guilty about the expression of a sense of relief. To many people it seems ungrateful and selfish. Work to help the person understand that relief certainly does not imply a lack of feeling for the person who died. The mourner's willingness to share components of the relief with you speaks of her trust in you. Through the process of entering into a supportive relationship with the griever, you become a catalyst for the restoration of meaning and purpose in his life.

Reconciliation

The final dimension of grief in a number of proposed models is often referred to as resolution, recovery, reestablishment, or reorganization. This dimension often suggests a total return to "normalcy" and yet in my personal as well as professional experience, everyone is changed by the experience of grief. For the mourner to assume that life will be exactly as it was prior to the death is unrealistic and potentially damaging. Recovery as understood by some persons, mourners and caregivers alike, is all too often seen erroneously as an absolute, a perfect state of reestablishment.

Reconciliation is a term I believe to be more expressive of what occurs as the person works to integrate the new reality of moving forward in life without the physical presence of the person who has died. What occurs is a renewed sense of energy and confidence, an ability to fully acknowledge the reality of the death, and the capacity to become reinvolved with the activities of living. Also an acknowledgement occurs that pain and grief are difficult yet necessary parts of life and living.

As the experience of reconciliation unfolds, the mourner recognizes that life will be different without the presence of the significant person who has died. A realization occurs that reconciliation is a process, not an event. Working through the emotional relationship with the person who has died and re-directing energy and initiative toward the future often take longer and involve more labor than most people are aware. We as human beings never "get over" our grief, but instead become reconciled to it.

We have noted that the course of mourning cannot be prescribed because it depends on many factors, such as the nature of the relationship with the person who died, the availability and helpfulness of a support system, the nature of the death, and the ritual or funeral experience. As a result, despite how much we now know about dimensions of the grief experience, they will take different forms with different people. One of the major factors influencing the mourner's movement toward reconciliation is that she be allowed to mourn in her own unique way and time.

Reconciliation is the dimension wherein the full reality of the death becomes a part of the mourner. Beyond an intellectual working through is an emotional and spiritual working through. What has been understood at the "head" level is now understood at the "heart" level—someone loved is dead. When a reminder such as holidays, anniversaries, or other special memories are triggered, the mourner experiences the intense pain inherent in grief, yet the duration and intensity of the pain is typically less severe as the healing of reconciliation occurs.

The pain of grief goes from being ever-present, sharp, and stinging to an acknowledged feeling of loss that has given rise to renewed meaning and purpose. The sense of loss does not completely disappear yet softens and the intense pangs of grief become less frequent. Hope for a continued life emerges as the griever is able to make commitments to the future, realizing that the dead person will never be forgotten, yet knowing that one's own life can and will move forward.

In the table on the following pages are criteria for reconciliation that are intended to give the reader some guidelines suggesting that the mourner has participated in the work of mourning and integrated the loss into his life.

The Companion's Helping Role. Movement toward reconciliation is draining and exhausting, not only for the mourner, but also for the helper who accompanies the person on the journey. In a general sense, being supportively present and helping the person gently mourn is the primary role of the companion. Grief is often so painful that people

◇◇◇◇◇◇◇◇◇◇◇◇◇◇◇◇◇◇◇◇◇◇◇◇◇◇◇◇◇◇◇◇

Criteria for reconciliation

Those persons who have worked with their grief to move toward the dimension of reconciliation will often demonstrate:

A recognition of the reality and finality of the death (in both the head and heart).

A return to stable eating and sleeping patterns that were present prior to the death.

A renewed sense of energy and personal well-being.

A subjective sense of release or relief from the person who has died (they have thoughts of the person, but are not preoccupied with these thoughts).

The capacity to enjoy experiences in life that should normally be enjoyable.

The establishment of new and healthy relationships.

The capacity to live a full life without feelings of guilt or lack of self-respect.

The capacity to organize and plan one's life toward the future.

The capacity to become comfortable with the way things are rather than attempting to make things as they were.

The capacity to being open to more change in one's life.

The awareness that one has allowed oneself to fully mourn and has survived.

The awareness that one does not "get over grief," but instead is able to acknowledge, "This is my new reality and I am ultimately the one who must work to create new meaning and purpose in my life."

The capacity to acknowledge new parts of one's self that have been discovered in the growth through one's grief.

The capacity to adjust to the new role changes that have resulted from the loss of the relationship.

The capacity to be compassionate with oneself when normal resurgences of intense grief occur (holidays, anniversaries, special occasions).

The capacity to acknowledge that the pain of loss is an inherent part of life that results from the ability to give and receive love.

WARNING: Remember, the mourner never arrives at some final destination or comes to a discrete end point. "Griefbursts" will continue forever.

Note: These criteria are intended to help you explore the mourner's Divine Momentum toward reconciliation. Not every person will illustrate each of these criteria; however, the majority of the criteria should be present for the person to be considered beyond ENCOUNTER (see page 128) with the new reality. Many bereaved persons will attempt to convince themselves and others that they are further along in the healing process than they really are. As a companion, you can support the mourner on the path to healing by remembering the mantra: "No rewards for speed, Divine Momentum, not attached to outcome."

will attempt to avoid it at all costs. While avoidance may bring temporary relief, the work of grief is ultimately something that cannot be postponed.

Establishing the hope of reconciliation is central to the ultimate unfolding of reconciliation. The majority of mourners experience a loss of confidence and esteem that leaves them questioning their capacity to heal. Those companions who are able to supportively embrace a willingness to hope and anticipate reconciliation assist mourners in movement toward their grief instead of away from it. This does not mean to deny pain, but a desire to "be with" those in their pain and helplessness, all the while knowing that all wounds get worse before they get better.

Just as we expect that mourners experience pain as a part of reconciliation, when we expect reconciliation, and know it is possible, we help the person acknowledge reconciliation as a realistic hope. However, if we as helpers somehow collaborate with those mourners who perceive that they will never move beyond the acute pain of their grief, we may well become a hindrance to their eventual healing.

Reconciliation from grief is normal. Yet, people need support, compassion, patience, perseverance, determination, and, perhaps most of all, hope and the belief in their capacity to heal. Part of the helping role is to serve as a catalyst that creates conditions outside the person and qualities within the person that make healing possible.

Just as the mourner's attitude toward the experience of grief influences the reconciliation process, the helper's attitude toward the healing environment invariably has a dramatic influence on the journey. To help people move toward reconciliation means to be open to your own experiences with grief while keeping the focus on those you are attempting to help. Obviously, if working on your grief ever becomes more important than working on their grief, you render yourself impotent as a companion.

As you work to support the reconciliation process, you do not impose your own direction on the content of what is explored; rather, you allow the direction of the mourner's experience to guide what you do and to help determine how you respond in supportive, life-enhancing ways. You appreciate the person as being independent from you and respect his right to determine the direction of the companioning relationship.

The process of helping another restore and renew herself calls upon all of your personal strengths as a helper. While working with people involved in the pain of grief is often difficult, slow, and wearing, the companioning experience also can be enriching and fulfilling in ways that go beyond words.

"Going to the woods and the wild place has little to do with recreation, and much to do with creation." —Wendell Berry

Wisdom Teaching Four:
Understand the Six Central Needs of Mourning

The death of someone loved changes the life of the mourner forever. And the movement from "before" to "after" is a naturally long, painful journey. From my own experience with loss as well as those of thousands of grieving people I have companioned over the years, I have learned that if we are to integrate loss into our lives, we cannot skirt the outside edges of our grief. Instead, we must journey all through it, sometimes meandering the side roads, sometimes plowing directly into its raw center.

A helpful concept for both the mourner and the companion is that of the six central needs of mourning. The mourner's awareness of these needs can help give a participative, action-oriented perception of grief instead of something passively experienced.

For those of you familiar with the literature on grief, you will note some similarity with other observers (Worden, Rando, Lindemann, Parkes and Weiss) in the perception of the mourner's needs. What follows is my take on these needs. Please note that following each of the six needs are questions for you, as a companion, to ask yourself as you witness the unfolding of the mourner's journey.

Throughout this chapter, you will also find a number of grief meditations related to the six needs of mourning. These reflections are excerpted from my book *The Journey Through Grief: Reflections on Healing*.

I often describe how the honoring of these needs by creating a "safe place" for the mourner to dose themselves on those needs is the essence of the companioning helping role. Remember—the focus is on "companioning," not "treating." What a privilege!

Mourning Need 1:
Acknowledge the Reality of the Death

This need of mourning involves gently confronting the reality that someone the mourner has cared about—given love to and received love from—has died. Whether the death was sudden or anticipated, acknowledging the full reality of the loss may occur over weeks, months, sometimes even years. As humans, we can know something in our heads (the cognitive reality) but not in our hearts (the affective reality).

The mourner may expect the dead person to come through the door or to call on the telephone. To survive, the mourner may try to push away the reality of the death at times. It is a sign of healthy discernment to want to protest the reality of death and recapture the physical presence of the person so dearly missed.

✧✧✧✧✧✧✧✧✧✧✧✧✧✧

"It's as if the realness of what has happened waits around a corner. I don't want to make the turn, yet I know I must. Slowly, I gather the courage to approach."

✧✧✧✧✧✧✧✧✧✧✧✧✧✧

The mourner will often move back and forth between protesting and encountering the reality of the death. She will often discover the need to replay events surrounding the death and confront memories both good and bad. This replay is a vital part of this need of mourning. It is as if each time the mourner talks it out (converts grief to mourning), the death is a little more real.

One moment the reality of the loss may be tolerable; another moment it may be unbearable. As a companion, your role is to be patient and gentle as the mourner re-visits this need. As the mourner experiences the safety of your mindfulness, he can and will give attention to this difficult need. Remember—this need of mourning, like the others that follow, will require your ongoing support and compassion. Your role is not to force the mourner to admit reality, but to create hospitable space for the mourner to authentically mourn.

We as humans come equipped with an organic capacity to slowly integrate loss into our lives. We can embrace grief and allow it to unfold into mourning. The reality that we as humans are capable of mourning tells us we are meant to gently acknowledge endings and integrate them into our lives. However, we cannot do this alone; we need loving companions.

✧✧✧✧✧✧✧✧✧✧✧✧✧✧

"To live into the future depends on my response to the reality of what I am experiencing. Temporarily, I need to create insulation from the full force of what I am coming to know. If I felt it all at once I might die. But feel it I must."

✧✧✧✧✧✧✧✧✧✧✧✧✧✧

Questions to Ask Yourself as a Companion:

- What is the mourner teaching me about where she is in the process of acknowledging the reality of the death?
- Is time a factor in where the mourner is in relation to this need?
- Do I need to respect the person's need to evade or push away some of the full sense of reality while she "doses" herself with the painful new reality?
- Is the mourner self-treating the pain of the reality of the loss in self-destructive patterns of behavior, such as alcohol or drug abuse, premature involvement in a new relationship, overeating, or impulsive spending as a means of avoiding this need?
- What can I as a companion do or be for this person to create a "safe place" to work on this need?

Mourning Need 2:
To Feel the Pain of the Loss

As I've mentioned, to be "bereaved" literally means "to be torn apart." When a person is torn apart by loss, mourning requires embracing the pain of the loss. Symptoms of pain and suffering are usually reflected in five domains—physical, emotional, cognitive, social and spiritual.

Let's look at how pain and suffering might "show up" for the mourner in each of these domains:

Physical: Bereavement naturally results in physical discomfort; the body responds to the stress of the encounter.

Emotional: Bereavement naturally results in emotional discomfort and a multitude of wave-like emotions may be experienced that demand comfort.

Cognitive: Bereavement naturally results in cognitive discomfort; thought processes are confused and memory is impaired.

Social: Bereavement naturally results in social discomfort; friends and family may withdraw and isolation may result.

Spiritual: Bereavement naturally results in spiritual discomfort; questions may arise such as, "Why go on living?"; "Will my life have meaning?"; "Where is God in this?"

For many people in a mourning-avoidant culture, it is easier to avoid, repress or deny the pain of grief than it is to confront it. Yet, it is in confronting one's pain and realizing it doesn't mean something is wrong that we ultimately integrate loss into our lives. To heal we must go to the wilderness of our souls.

❖❖❖❖❖❖❖❖❖❖❖❖❖❖

"I may try to protect myself from my sadness by not talking about my loss. I may even secretly hope that the person who died will come back if I don't talk about it. Yet, as difficult as it is, I must feel it to heal it."

❖❖❖❖❖❖❖❖❖❖❖❖❖❖

The opposite of embracing pain is often demonstrated by attempts to stay "in control." Underlying that controlling impulse is anxiety and fear—the fear that the mourner will have to experience pain in any or all of the five domains noted above.

If the mourner accepts that she cannot go around the pain of loss, then she may discover the courage (i.e., "the ability to do what one believes is right, despite the fact that others may strongly and persuasively disagree") to relax into the pain, and herein lies the paradox. Trying to avoid, repress or deny the pain of grief makes the mourner an opponent of the journey and creates more chronic states of anxiety and depression.

Control appears to be one of North Americans' favorite ways of running from grief and loss. We are so high on control that it has become an internalized illusion that we may think we can let go of control by simply wanting to. In other words, we think we can control relinquishing control! Human beings in grief do not let go of control; human beings in grief let go of the belief that we have control. Spiritual maturity in grief is attained when the mourner embraces a paradox—to live in the state of both encounter and surrender while simultaneously "working at" and "surrendering" to the journey.

As the mourner comes to know this paradox, she can very slowly, with no rewards for speed, discover the soothing of her soul. Many mourners have taught me that they actually find themselves wrapped in a gentle peace—the peace of living at once in the encounter (the "grief work") and the surrender (embracing the mystery of not understanding).

"The grief within me has its own heartbeat. It has its own life, its own song. Part of me wants to resist the rhythms of my grief. Yet, as I surrender to the song, I learn to listen deep within myself."

In many Eastern cultures, aging, illness and death are seen and experienced each and every day. When people live in daily contact with these realities, they tend not to deny that life involves pain and suffering. As Western culture has gained the capacity to limit pain and suffering, our culture tends to encourage the denial of pain. Advances in medicine and ever-increasing technology to lengthen lifespan have, without doubt, improved the levels of physical comfort for many North Americans.

However—this is when a shift in perception seems to have taken place—as pain and suffering have become less visible or have been relegated to behind closed doors, they are no longer perceived as an intrinsic part of the nature of being human, but instead seen as a sign that something has gone wrong.

Through no fault of their own, many mourners misunderstand the role of pain and suffering. If they openly express their feelings of grief, misinformed friends and family members often advise them to "carry on" or "let go." If, on the other hand, they remain "strong" and "in control," they may well be congratulated for "doing well" with their grief.

Many people surrounding the mourner want them to stay in control of their grief as a form of self-protection. We control because we are afraid of the pain of grief. It hurts to embrace the depths of the loss. It hurts to acknowledge our mortality and to be humbled by our life losses. As a companion to people in grief, you must become acquainted not only with the pain of others, but your own pain. Otherwise you will unconsciously want to "fix" people in pain, and not create hospitality for them to "dose" themselves with this need.

Yes, an essential part of your helping role is to help the mourner "dose" the pain of the loss. In other words, the mourner cannot (nor should she try to) overload herself with the hurt all at one time. In fact, sometimes your role may be to distract the mourner from the pain of the loss, while at other times you will need to create a "safe place" for the mourner to move toward the pain. Dose the pain: yes! Deny the pain: no!

Authentic companions always remember that the pain of grief is something to be experienced in "doses," not some event that is to be "overcome" or have "closure" on. Pain within the five domains of loss will ebb and flow for months and years. The creation of sacred space on your part as a companion demands patience, support and compassion.

Questions to Ask Yourself As a Companion:

• Does the person understand the role of pain and suffering in integrating loss into life?
• What symptoms of care-eliciting emotions and behaviors has this person had within the five domains outlined above?
• Does the person demonstrate self-compassion and patience in "dosing" herself with the pain of the loss?

• What can I as a companion do or be for this person to create a "safe place" to work on this need?

Mourning Need 3:
To Remember the Person Who Died

This need is anchored in helping the mourner pursue a relationship of memory with the person who died. As Kierkegaard noted, "While life must be lived forward, it can only be understood backwards." In contrast, many people around the mourner often believe their primary helping role is to get the mourner to "let go" and efficiently move forward.

As a companion your role is to help the mourner feel affirmed in having an altered yet continued relationship of memory. Memories—good, bad and indifferent, dreams reflecting the significance of the relationship and objects that link the mourner to the person who died (such as photos, souvenirs, clothing, etc.)—are examples of some of the things that give testimony to a different form of continued relationship.

"The essence of finding meaning in the future is not to forget the past, as I have been told, but instead to embrace my past. For it is in listening to the music of the past that I can sing in the present and dance into the future."

For many people, the process of beginning to embrace memories often begins with a funeral or memorial service. The ceremony can help create Divine Momentum to remember the person who died and help "hold up" the value of the life that was lived. The memories embraced during the time of the ceremony help set the tone for the changed nature of the relationship.

The mantra of "no rewards for speed" can help remind you that integrating memories can be a very slow and, at times, painful process. As a companion, part of your helping role is to encourage the awesome power of "telling the story" over and over again.

Many mourners will tell you of experiences in which people around them have tried to take their mourning away from them. They may have had some well-meaning friends and family tell them to take down all the photos of the person who died. They may have been told to "keep busy" so they don't think about the person who died. The mourner herself may think that avoiding memories would be better for her. And why not? We are all living in a culture that teaches us to move away from instead of toward our grief.

In contrast, your companioning role is to help the mourner remember thoughts, feelings and the essence of what was a vital part of her life. Whatever the memories are, they must be listened to and respected. As you support the "telling of the story," you make easier the shift from a relationship of presence to a relationship of memory.

Obviously, not every mourner has pleasant memories. This reality makes integrating this need more naturally complicated. Yet, to ignore painful or ambivalent memories is to prevent healing from taking place. In the safety of your non-judgmental, empathetic relationship and with the right timing and pacing, the mourner can explore these memories with you. If the mourner represses or denies these memories when they exist, she risks carrying on underlying sadness or anger into her future.

❖❖❖❖❖❖❖❖❖❖❖❖❖❖

"I can release the pain that touches my memories, but only if I remember them. I can release my grief, but only if I express it. Memories and grief must have a heart to hold them."

❖❖❖❖❖❖❖❖❖❖❖❖❖❖

Memories and grief must have a heart to hold them. Remembering the past makes hoping for the future possible. As a companion you have the honor of being present to the mourner as she discovers that the essence of finding meaning in the future is not to forget the past, but to embrace the past.

Questions to Ask Yourself As a Companion:

• Where is this person in shifting the relationship from one of presence to one of memory?

- Has this person had experience with being told to "let go" of the past? If so, how has this influenced the grief experience?
- What ways does this person give honor to a relationship of memory?
- Is the person resisting any shift in the relationship and trying to maintain the relationship as one of presence?
- What can I as a companion do or be for this person to create a "safe place" to work on this need?

Mourning Need 4:
To Develop a New Self-Identity

This need relates to the evolution of a new self-identity based on a life without the physical presence of the person who has died. Part of every human being's self-identity or self-perception comes from the relationships we have with other people. When someone with whom the grieving person has a relationship dies, her self-identity, or the way she sees herself, naturally changes.

The mourner may have gone from being a "wife" or "husband" to a "widow" or "widower." The mourner may have gone from being a "parent" to a "bereaved parent." The way he defines himself and the way society defines him is changed.

The mourner has lost a "mirror" that helped her know who she was and how she had meaning in her life. A vital need is to have companions who can empathize with and understand how she doesn't simply wake up one day after the death and know who she is. Redefining a new sense of self is a slow process, not an event in time.

◇◇◇◇◇◇◇◇◇◇◇◇◇

"Now I realize: I knew myself so little. This death has forced me to become reacquainted with myself. I must slow down and listen."

◇◇◇◇◇◇◇◇◇◇◇◇◇

A death often requires the mourner to take on new roles that had been filled by the person who died. After all, someone still has to take out the garbage, someone still has to buy the groceries, someone still has to balance the checkbook. The mourner confronts his changed identity every time he does something that used to be done by the person who died.

This is very hard work and, at times, can leave the mourner feeling very drained of emotional, physical and spiritual energy.

She may sometimes feel childlike as she struggles with her changing identity and loss of "mirror." She may feel a temporarily heightened dependence on others and experience feelings of helplessness, frustration, inadequacy and fear. These feelings can be overwhelming and frightening, yet they are a natural response to this important need of mourning.

There is a powerful draw to want to have back one's "old self," but with the loss of the mirror, that old self is gone forever. Now, being temporarily lost in the wilderness of grief is the familiar but naturally uncomfortable place. Slowly, over time and with gentle companioning, the mourner can work toward discovery of a new self. As the mourner experiences being "betwixt and between," you can bring your open heart, compassion and hospitality to the helping journey.

Questions to Ask Yourself As a Companion:

• Where is this mourner in the evolution of a new self-identity?
• Is time an influence on where this person is in working on this need?
• What are the role changes that this person is experiencing as a result of this death?
• Are role models—others who have gone through similar experiences—available to the mourner?
• What can I as a companion do or be for this person to create a "safe place" to work on this need?

"When I have a commitment and longing to find my changed self, I have an alternative to the constant, blinding pain of the loss. Discovering my changed me clears a space to discover new life. I have something to turn toward instead of away from. I have something to cry out for that releases my inner tension. I have something that is authentic, real: It is the life that breaks through my loneliness, with a direction and power of its own. Welcome home."

Mourning Need 5:
To Search for Meaning

This need relates to renewing one's resources for life and living after having been "torn apart." When someone loved dies, the mourner naturally questions the meaning and purpose of life. She may question her philosophy of life and explore religious and spiritual values as she works on this need.

She may discover herself searching for meaning in her continued living as she asks "why?" and "how?" questions. "Why did this happen now, in this way?" "How will I go on living?" The "why?" questions often precede the "how?" questions in this unfolding process. This search for a reason to go on living is a vital part of grief work and requires an expenditure of physical, emotional and spiritual energy.

The person who died was part of the mourner. He must now mourn a death not only outside of himself, but inside of himself as well. He also mourns for all of the dreams, hopes and unfulfilled expectations held for the person and their relationship.

At times, overwhelming sadness and loneliness may be her constant companions. She may feel that when the person died, part of her died, too. And now she is faced with finding some meaning in going on with her life even though she feels so empty and alone.

The death of someone loved invites mourners to explore their worldviews—that set of beliefs people have about how the universe functions and what place they, as individuals, occupy therein. Some studies have observed that many people in modern Western culture tend to travel through life believing that the world is essentially a nice place in which to live, that life is mostly fair, and that they are basically good people who deserve to have good things happen to them. In other words, this is a common worldview.

But when a death, particularly an untimely or tragic death, comes, the pain and suffering that result undermine these beliefs and can make it very difficult to continue living this happy life. The death can have an overwhelming impact as the mourner may lose faith in his basic beliefs about the world being benevolent and fair. The result is that through the search for meaning, pain and suffering are intensified.

So, where does the mourner begin her search for meaning and renewal of resources for life and living? For many people in grief, the search begins with their religious or spiritual traditions. The "torn apart" mourner may doubt her faith and have spiritual conflicts and questions racing through her head and heart. Obviously, this is a normal part of the journey toward renewal.

"I must encounter my questions, my doubts, my fears. There is richness in these domains. As I explore them, I don't reinforce my tensions but instead release them. In this way I transcend my grief and discover new life beyond anything my heart could ever have comprehended. Oh, the gentleness of new life."

For example, in the Judeo-Christian tradition, a foundational belief is that the universe was created by a good and just God. The death of someone loved naturally challenges many mourners' belief in the goodness of God and the belief that the world is essentially a nice place in which to live. Therefore, as an open-hearted companion, you should not be shocked or surprised to hear mourners say things like, "I'm not sure I'd mind it if I didn't wake up tomorrow." This kind of comment is often an invitation to the wilderness of his grief. Now, the question becomes, can you accept the invitation without feeling the need to deny his reality?

When such beliefs or long-standing worldviews are initially challenged in early grief, there is often little if anything to replace them right away. This is a part of the "suspension" or "void" that grief initiates—an absence of belief that precedes any renewal of belief.

There is for many mourners a profound lack of sense of direction or future purpose, particularly since the mourner's meaning in life as well as his hopes, dreams and plans for the future were invested heavily in a relationship that no longer exists. In sum, the mourner may teach you he is experiencing the "cosmic" nature of grief, wherein the world no longer makes sense in the way it did before the death.

Each mourner's worldview and beliefs, once impacted by the death of someone loved, evolve into a state of reconstruction before she can become re-engaged in life and living. This re-emergence can occur if the mourner has companions who can be fully present to her in the depths of the wilderness experience. As Martin Luther King, Jr. once noted, "What does not destroy me, makes me stronger." Yet, that strength does not come quickly or efficiently.

Bringing one's torn-apart world back together takes time, loving companions and humility—that virtue that helps us humans when we face powerlessness. A vital part of helping people search for meaning is encouraging them to mourn without any pressure to have answers to profound "meaning of life" questions.

"I deserve to be proud of my search for meaning in life after the death of someone I love. Grief confronts me with the reality that life is now. Today. I can demonstrate the value in my life and the lives of those who have died by living them fully."

Creating sacred space where mourners can hurt and eventually find meaning in continued living are not mutually exclusive. Actually, the need to openly mourn and slowly discover renewed meaning in continued living can and do naturally blend into each other, with the former giving way to the latter as healing unfolds. Our universal calling as human beings is to be the most loving people we can possibly be. In sharing your gift of helping mourners search for meaning after the death of someone loved, you may well have found your calling.

Questions to Ask Yourself As a Companion:

• Where is this person in the process of renewing resources for life and living?
• What were this person's religious, spiritual, and philosophical beliefs about life and death prior to this loss?

177

- Has the loss altered those beliefs? If so, how?
- Does the mourner give himself permission to explore previously held beliefs or worldviews?
- What can I as a companion do or be for this person to create a "safe place" to work on this need?

Mourning Need 6: To Receive Ongoing Support From Others

This need acknowledges the reality that the mourner will need support long after the event of the death. Because mourning is a "dosed" process that unfolds over time, support must be available months and even years after the death. The quality and quantity of support the mourner receives is a major influence on the capacity to integrate the loss into her life and renew resources for living.

Unfortunately, because our society places so much emphasis on returning to "normal" within a linear period of time, many bereaved people are abandoned shortly after the death. When possible, an essential ingredient of your companioning role is to support the mourner not only in the period of acute grief, but over the long-term.

❖❖❖❖❖❖❖❖❖❖❖❖

"I heal, in part, by allowing others to express their love for me. By choosing to invite others into my journey, I move toward health and healing. If I hide from others, I hide from healing."

❖❖❖❖❖❖❖❖❖❖❖❖

To be truly helpful, the people who make up the support system must appreciate the impact the death has had and is having on the mourner. They must understand that in order to slowly reconcile the death, the mourner must be allowed—even encouraged—to mourn long after the death. And they must perceive mourning not as an enemy to be vanquished but as a necessity to be experienced as a result of having loved.

By its very nature, the experience of grief can be very lonely. Healing, in part, comes about through staying connected to support systems and the outside world. As previously noted under Wisdom Teaching

Two, part of your companioning role is anchored in creating Divine Momentum to help activate effective support in the life of the mourner.

As you companion the mourner, you will learn about the support he may or may not receive from individual family members or friends, from faith communities or other groups that are a part of his life. You will learn that some mourners openly seek and accept support while others are more likely to have difficulty opening themselves to the support that is available to them. Some mourners will teach you that stigmatized circumstances of death (suicide, homicide, AIDS) have impacted their capacity to receive support. Often, the greater the stigma, the less support is available and the more risk for what is called mutual pretense: where people around the mourner know what has happened but believe they should not talk about it with the survivor.

"I need not instinctively know what to do or how to be with my grief. I can reach out to others who have walked this path before. I learn that to ultimately heal, I must touch and be touched by the experiences of those who have gone before me. These people can offer me hope, inner strength, and the gift of love."

Obviously, certain days or times of the year will call out for much-needed support for the mourner. For example, birthdays, holidays, change of seasons, the date of the death, one's own birthday can all trigger griefbursts—heightened periods of sadness and loss that benefit from ongoing support. A number of cultures have a dedicated "Day of the Dead" to, in part, provide the benefit of support during a naturally difficult time.

A vital part of the companioning role is to be among those whom the mourner can depend upon to understand that grief and mourning's impact continues long after society deems appropriate. Demonstrating this sensitivity in your way of being in the world and in your responsiveness to the mourner will reflect this awareness.

- Does the person have ongoing support available? If so, from whom?
- Does the person feel abandoned by any person or group that she hoped to receive support from?
- Are there any stigmatized circumstances surrounding the death that put the mourner at risk for not receiving support?
- Is the person willing and able to accept support?
- Are there some specific days or times of the year where the person would benefit from additional support?
- What can I as a companion do or be for this person to create a "safe place" to get this need met?

The Importance of the Six Central Needs of Mourning

I cannot overemphasize the importance of how you, as a companion, can benefit from a working knowledge of these six needs of mourning.

Essentially, this is your helping role job description. As you give attention to these needs, the mourner will have a safe place to dose herself on these needs and, over time and through the work of mourning, begin to see a softening of the symptoms that reflect her special needs.

Grief is real and it does not simply go away as time passes. Experiencing grief and mourning is often equivalent to journeying through an unknown territory rife with an overwhelming sense of pain and loss. And yet, in companioning people through these six needs of mourning, you have the opportunity to be a catalyst for healing.

"When we walk to the edge of all the light we have and take a step into the darkness of the unknown, we must believe one of two things will happen—there will be something solid for us to stand upon, or we will be taught to fly." —Anonymous

Wisdom Teaching Five:
Embrace the Transformative Nature of Grief

A major theme of this book is that mourners are well-served to become friendly with the emotions of grief. When someone we have given love to and received love from dies, we begin a journey of the heart. An open heart that is grieving is a "well of reception;" it is moved entirely by what it has perceived. Having companions with whom to authentically mourn is an opportunity to embrace that open heart in ways that allow for and encourage transformation.

To be torn apart by the death of someone loved casts us into the wilderness. Daily routines are thrown into disarray. Our life stories are forever changed. We search and yearn for the return of the one who died. We feel joyless and wonder if we can go on without her. We feel overwhelmed and helpless as we confront the reality that we cannot bring him back to life. We want to be able to keep on loving her in the here and now. We rightly protest, with all the energy we can muster, when others tell us we must "let go."

Over time we (I hope) learn that feeling the pain of grief does not mean that we are sick. We learn to depathologize the journey into grief. We learn that while we live in a culture that would prefer a quick fix for our grief, we must slow down and surrender.

We must surrender to the energies of grief and descend into and through the experience. In so doing, we create conditions that allow and encourage something new to arise from within us. With loving companions, we rise from the depths of our grief and discover unexpected healing and transformation. This healing occurs not by separating ourselves from the pain, but by attending to it. Yes, Helen Keller was right when she observed, "The only way to the other side is through."

Creating Hope for Healing in Your
Fellow Human Beings

To companion fellow mourners is to open your heart to compassion and to bring hope for both healing and transformation. I have discovered in my thirty years as a grief counselor that a large part of the hope that comes from the journey through grief is the capacity to live and love fully until we die.

Earlier in this book I defined hope as "an expectation of a good that is yet to be." Living with hope in the midst of grief is believing that as mourners, we can and will go on to discover a continued life that can be rich in living and loving fully. I believe that when we embrace the attitude that everyone is a spiritual being here for a sacred purpose—naturally encountering some pain of grief along the path—we can view those around us through a filter of companionship. As emphasized throughout this resource, companionship is anchored in patience, compassion and gentleness.

As companions, we acknowledge and respect that grief is life-changing. When people rise up from the wilderness of grief, they, and all of us, are not the same as when we entered the wilderness. Obviously, there is no way we could be.

Transformation literally means an entire change in form. Many fellow travelers in grief have said to me, "I am a totally different person than I was before." Yes, they are indeed different. Their inner form has changed. They have often grown in their wisdom, in their gratitude, and in their compassion.

"Only he who suffers can be the guide and healer of the suffering."—Thomas Mann

As companions, we must remind ourselves that growth resulting from the death of someone loved is something most people would prefer to avoid. Though grief can indeed transform into growth, neither you nor I would instinctively seek out the pain of loss in an effort to experience this growth.

While I have come to believe that our greatest gifts often come from our wounds, these are not wounds we masochistically go looking for. Having acknowledged this reality to understand how transformation in grief occurs when people have safe and trusted companions for the journey, let us explore some aspects of growth in grief. But what precisely do I mean by growth in grief? I mean many things, the most important of which I will explore here.

❖❖❖❖❖❖❖❖❖❖❖❖❖❖❖

"Loss provides an opportunity to take inventory of our lives, to reconsider priorities, and to determine new directions."
—Gerald L. Sittser

❖❖❖❖❖❖❖❖❖❖❖❖❖❖❖

Growth Means Change

Again, we as human beings are forever changed by the death of someone we love. To talk about resolving someone's grief, which denotes a return to "the way things were" before the death, doesn't allow for the transformation I have both personally experienced and witnessed in others who have mourned. Mourning is not an end, but a beginning.

The mourner may discover that she has developed new attitudes. She may be more sensitive to the feelings and circumstances of others, especially those suffering from loss. She may have new insights that shape the way she lives her new life. She may realize that each person in life is unique and irreplaceable. She may embrace the reality that while she cannot bring back the dead, she can give the dead a place in her heart. She may discover that she can integrate cherished memories made in love with new experiences of giving and receiving love. And she may discover new passions that invite her to live fully until she dies.

As companions who use the concept of growth, we can go beyond the traditional medical model of bereavement care that teaches that the helping goal is to return the bereaved person to a homeostatic state of being. A return to inner balance doesn't reflect how I, or the mourners who have taught me about their grief journeys, are forever changed by the experience of loss. In using the word growth, we acknowledge and respect the changes mourning brings about.

As companions, we are not frightened by the reality that no one ever totally completes the mourning journey. People who think you get over grief are often continually striving to "pull it all together," while at the same time they feel that something is missing. The paradox is that the more anyone tries to "resolve" his own grief, the more his spirit, or life force, will protest. After all, resolution is an unachievable goal.

◇◇◇◇◇◇◇◇◇◇◇◇◇

"Growth is an erratic forward movement: two steps forward, one step back. Remember that and be very gentle with yourself."
—Julia Cameron

"If you are seeking a time when you will be finished, you will never be done."
—Tibetan saying

◇◇◇◇◇◇◇◇◇◇◇◇◇

I'll never forget the participant in one of my small group retreats who wrote me the following note upon her return home:

I know that in my own work of grief and mourning (dating back to childhood), I have always judged myself and secretly believed I was "wrong" for not being able to "resolve" my sense of loss and bring my various grief experiences to completion… I continued to judge myself, to perceive myself as deficient or "less than." The concept of reconciliation freed me from the need to judge myself. It also permitted me to experience a remarkable sense of healing in my sense of "self" and in my belief in my ability to "handle" events in appropriate ways.

The woman's experience nicely illustrates how there is no end-point to the grief journey. Nor does the mourner return to a previous "inner balance" or "normal" but instead eventually, with no rewards for speed, achieves a new inner balance and a new normal. Yes, growth means a new inner balance.

Growth Means Exploring Assumptions About Life

The death of someone you have opened your heart to invites the mourner to look at assumptions about life. Grief invites the mourner to look deeply into the way things are and what is really important. Life is brief. We are here for a very short period of time. Grief reminds us of this, not only in a head way, but in a heart way. This gift of grace comes from the confrontation of death, not running away from it.

❖❖❖❖❖❖❖❖❖❖❖❖❖

"Life is change. Growth is optional. Choose wisely."
—Karen Kaiser Clark

❖❖❖❖❖❖❖❖❖❖❖❖❖

Yes, grief has a way of transforming the mourner's assumptions, values, and priorities. What she may have formerly thought of as being important—a nice house, a new car—may not matter any longer. The job that the mourner used to be enamored by may now seem trivial. The mourner may now value material goods and status less and relationships more.

For many people, exploring psycho-spiritual questions like "Where is God in all of this?" can be a long and arduous part of the journey. Yet ultimately, exploring these assumptions about life and death can make these assumptions richer and more life-affirming. Every loss in life calls out for a new search for meaning, including a natural struggle with spiritual concerns, often transforming the mourner's vision of her God and her faith life. Yes, grief means exploring assumptions about life.

Growth Means Utilizing One's Potential

The encounter of grief awakens many mourners to the importance of utilizing their potential. In some ways, death loss seems to free the potential within, to invite the discovery of one's gifts and to be interpersonally effective in relationships with others.

Important questions such as, "Who am I?" "What am I meant to do with my life?" often naturally arise during grief. Answering them inspires a hunt. Someone wise once observed, "Those who do not search, do not find." Mourning invites such a search.

In part, seeking purpose means living inside the questions. Beyond that, it means being able to say, "Does my life really matter?" Rather than dragging the mourner down, grief may ultimately lift the mourner up. Then it becomes up to the mourner to embrace and creatively express her new-found potential.

◇◇◇◇◇◇◇◇◇◇◇◇◇

"Untapped potential is the difference between where a person is now and where he or she can be." —Bo Bennett

◇◇◇◇◇◇◇◇◇◇◇◇◇

Until the mourner makes peace with his purpose and uses his potential, he may not experience contentment in his life. Joy and gratitude can come when the mourner knows in his heart that he is using his potential—in his work or in his free time or in his relationships with friends and family.

I believe that grief's call to use one's potential is why many mourners go on to help others in grief. She doesn't necessarily need to become a grief therapist. She may volunteer to help out with a grief support group or a local hospice. She may reach out to a neighbor struggling or devote more time to her children or grandchildren. Helping others in some way, shape or form is for many mourners a vital part of discovering their gifts and putting them to use. Yes, growth means utilizing one's potential.

Growth Means Living and Loving Again Arises From Within

Sorrow is an inseparable dimension of our human experience. We suffer after a loss because we are human. And in our suffering, we are transformed. In opening to our broken hearts we open ourselves to the rebirth of living and loving again until we too die.

While it hurts to suffer lost love, the alternative is apathy. Apathy literally means the inability to suffer, and it results in a lifestyle that avoids human relationships to avoid suffering. Some mourners choose to die a long time before they stop breathing. They have no more promises to keep, no more people to love, no more places to go. It is as if the souls of these people have already died. It's true that death may not be the greatest loss in life; the greatest loss in life may be what dies inside you while you live.

No matter how much we have loved the person who has died, the purpose of authentic mourning is to rediscover the capacity to keep living and loving. While our love for the dead goes on, if we love the dead to the exclusion of the living we join the living dead.

I truly believe that those who have died before us live on through our capacity to keep living and loving with wide open hearts. When we honor the love they have given us by loving our family and friends, our dead live on. If we stop living and loving, the love they gifted to us serves no continued purpose.

No matter how deep one's grief or how anguished one's soul, there still comes a responsibility to live and love fully until we die. To do so is to give testimony to the transformative yet restorative nature of grief and mourning.

Companioning the Mourner's Transformed Soul

Yes, souls are transformed by the death of someone loved. Essentially, grief work is soul work. What people in mourning need most is to be lovingly companioned, to feel and experience that those who walk with them are willing and able to tolerate the painful work of mourning, to be totally present to them, and give attention to their transformation and reconstruction.

As a responsible rebel, you know that there is no wisdom in giving out any "It's time for you to get back to normal" messages. Out of your capacity to suspend and honor the journey, you will witness the at times imperceptible yet very real transformation of a mourner's heart and soul.

Honoring this transformation is grounded in your awareness of the "wisdom teachings" outlined in Part Two of this book—misconceptions, unique influences, dimensions of response, and six central needs of mourning. I believe these foundational wisdom teachings will help you create Divine Momentum for the mourner to not only mourn well but also live well and love well.

❖❖❖❖❖❖❖❖❖❖❖❖❖❖❖❖❖❖❖❖❖❖❖❖❖❖❖

"Problems do not go away. They must be worked through or else they remain, forever a barrier to the growth and development of the spirit." —M. Scott Peck

❖❖❖❖❖❖❖❖❖❖❖❖❖❖❖❖❖❖❖❖❖❖❖❖❖❖❖

A Final Word

It was Thomas Moore who observed, "Our science and technologies approach life as a problem to be solved." This made me reflect on the reality that our therapies approach grief as a pathology to be cured. My hope is that you agree with me that it is time to face the need for change in how we support each other in grief.

To experience and embrace the pain of loss is just as much a part of life as to experience the joy of love. As it should be, thoughts, feelings, and behaviors that result from the death of a person who has been loved are impossible to ignore. The experience of grief is very powerful. As we encounter personal loss in our lives, we have the opportunity to make a willful choice of how we are going to use the pain of the grief—whether we are going to channel it to make our lives better or worse.

Companioning as a Reflection of Love

At the very heart of companioning is the need to acknowledge each other as equals, not as "therapist" and "patient." What makes us all equals is that we are all human beings who will come to know the pain and suffering that emanates from the loss of those we have loved. We also need each other.

Companioning can only take place among equals. If anyone believes she has superior knowledge of another's journey into grief, this belief destroys the foundation of a relationship anchored in unconditional love. Those who project what I call "superior expertise" can't help but "treat" the mourner, and usually—consciously or unconsciously— try to achieve some variation of "closure." When we see each other as equals, we do not misuse each other. Acknowledging each other as equals is a reflection of love.

Companioning is also about compassionate curiosity. When we support each other with this humility, we open our hearts to another human being. Curiosity encourages us to take off our professional masks and create sacred, hospitable free space for the mourner. It takes time and conscious effort to create this space in a mourning-avoidant culture. Compassionate curiosity encourages us to extend ourselves rather than withdraw into our own worlds. Yes, companioning invites us to extend ourselves, open our hearts wide, be still and really listen.

Companioning also depends on our willingness to reject grief as a pathology and not think of our role as eradicating emotional and spiritual suffering. We must surrender to the wilderness to be willing to wander into the mystery. We have to expect chaos, confusion, disorder, and even despair. So-called "negative" emotions and experiences are not dangerous. Messiness has its place. Grief loss and change always start with confusion. We can't be companions if we refuse to be confused. Integration of loss often occurs in the space of not knowing. We don't need to be joined at the head with a mourner; we need to be joined at the heart.

Just as we are faced with choices in our personal experiences with loss, we also are faced with choices in our life's work as companions to those in grief. We can choose to help people avoid the work of their grief, or we can support and accompany people as they fully enter into their grief. If we are able to achieve the latter of these choices, chances are we can become catalysts for Divine Momentum and a renewed sense of meaning and purpose in the lives of our fellow human beings.

I have always been drawn to Robert Frost's classic poem that, in part, reads: "Two roads diverged in a wood, and I—I took the one less traveled by, and that has made all the difference." Companioning is not a technique or a therapy, it is a philosophy and a discipline for every hour, every day, every week, every month, and every year of your life. For me, the "road taken" is:

• Finding passion and purpose in ministering to those in grief.
• Attending to those things in life that give my life richness and purpose.

- Having gratitude each day for my family and friends.
- Trying to fulfill my destiny, by developing my soul's potential.
- Striving to "give back" what others have given to me.
- By observing what is requesting my attention, and giving attention to it.
- Going out into nature and having gratitude for the beauty of the universe.
- Praying that I'm living "on purpose" and using my gifts whether by writing a book, teaching a workshop, or caring for my children.
- Going through my own struggles with grief and realizing that it is working through these wounds that helps unite me with others.

Every day we each have the opportunity to be companions, to listen with our hearts, and to be curious rather than certain. Thank you so much for taking time to read this book. I hope you choose to see your heart opening to people experiencing grief. When your heart is open, you are receptive to what life brings you, both happy and sad. By "staying open" you create a pathway to living life fully until you die.

Companioning the Dying
A Soulful Guide for Caregivers

By Greg Yoder
Foreword by Alan D. Wolfelt

If you work with the dying in your career or as a volunteer, or if you are a family member or friend to someone who is dying, this book presents you with a caregiving philosophy that will help you know how to respond, and what to do with your own powerful emotions. Most of all, this book will help you feel at peace about both your own role as caregiver and the dying person's experience—no matter how it unfolds.

Based on the assumption that all dying experiences belong not to the caregivers but to those who are dying—and that there is no such thing as a "good death" or a "bad death," *Companioning The Dying* helps readers bring a respectful, nonjudgmental presence to the dying while liberating them from self-imposed or popular expectations to say or do the right thing.

Written with candor and wit by hospice counselor Greg Yoder (who has companioned several hundred dying people and their families), *Companioning The Dying* exudes a compassion and a clarity that can only come from intimate work with the dying. The book teaches through real-life stories that will resonate with both experienced clinical professionals as well as laypeople in the throes of caring for a dying loved one.

ISBN 1-879651-42-4 • hardcover • 176 pages • $29.95

Companion
PRESS

All publications can be ordered by mail from:
Companion Press
3735 Broken Bow Road • Fort Collins, CO 80526
(970) 226-6050 • Fax 1-800-922-6051
www.centerforloss.com

Companioning at a Time of Perinatal Loss
A Guide for Nurses, Physicians, Social Workers and Chaplains in the Hospital Setting

By Jane Heustis & Marcia Meyer Jenkins
Foreword by Alan D. Wolfelt, Ph.D.

The OB unit is the only hospital environment where life begins and, sometimes, tragically ends. Staff must alternate masks of comedy and tragedy as they care for the estimated 2-4 percent of deliveries that end in the death of a baby. Many OB caregivers feel unprepared to handle the intensity of perinatal loss. Most hospitals have bereavement care standards but offer little instruction in following them. Written by seasoned support nurses, Companioning at a Time of Perinatal Loss outlines a framework for bereavement care in the obstetrical arena. Based on Dr. Alan Wolfelt's principles of companioning, it describes loss from the family's perspective, defines the caregiver's role, offers bedside strategies and reviews the work of mourning in the weeks and months after. Real-life stories teach what is important during times of intense sorrow.

ISBN 1-879651-47-5 • 144 pages • softcover • $19.95
(plus additional shipping and handling)

Companion
PRESS

All publications can be ordered by mail from:
Companion Press
3735 Broken Bow Road • Fort Collins, CO 80526
(970) 226-6050 • Fax 1-800-922-6051
www.centerforloss.com

Understanding Your Grief
Ten Essential Touchstones for Finding Hope and Healing Your Heart

One of North America's leading grief educators, Dr. Alan Wolfelt has written many books about healing in grief. This book is his most comprehensive, covering the most important lessons that mourners have taught him in his three decades of working with the bereaved.

In compassionate, everyday language, Understanding Your Grief explains the important difference between grief and mourning and explores the mourner's need to gently acknowledge the death and embrace the pain of the loss. This important book also reveals the many factors that make each person's grief unique and the myriad of normal thoughts and feelings the mourner might have. Alan's philosophy of finding "companions" in grief versus "treaters" is explored. Dr. Wolfelt also offers suggestions for good self-care.

Throughout, Dr. Wolfelt affirms the readers' rights to be compassionate with themselves, lean on others for help, and trust in their innate ability to heal.

ISBN 1-879651-35-1 • 176 pages • softcover • $14.95
(plus additional shipping and handling)

Companion
PRESS

All Dr. Wolfelt's publications can be ordered by mail from:
Companion Press
3735 Broken Bow Road • Fort Collins, CO 80526
(970) 226-6050 • Fax 1-800-922-6051
www.centerforloss.com

The Understanding Your Grief Journal
Exploring the Ten Essential Touchstones

Writing can be a very effective form of mourning, or expressing your grief outside yourself. And it is through mourning that you heal in grief.

The Understanding Your Grief Journal is a companion workbook to *Understanding Your Grief.* Designed to help mourners explore the many facets of their unique grief through journaling, this compassionate book interfaces with the ten essential touchstones. Throughout, journalers are asked specific questions about their own unique grief journeys as they relate to the touchstones and are provided with writing space for the many questions asked.

Purchased as a set together with *Understanding Your Grief,* this journal is a wonderful mourning tool and safe place for those in grief. It also makes an ideal grief support group workbook.

ISBN 1-879651-39-4 • 112 pages • softcover • $14.95
(plus additional shipping and handling)

Companion
PRESS

All Dr. Wolfelt's publications can be ordered by mail from:
Companion Press
3735 Broken Bow Road • Fort Collins, CO 80526
(970) 226-6050 • Fax 1-800-922-6051
www.centerforloss.com

The Journey Through Grief: Reflections On Healing
Second Edition

This revised, second edition of *The Journey Through Grief* takes Dr. Wolfelt's popular book of reflections and adds space for guided journaling, asking readers thoughtful questions about their unique mourning needs and providing room to write responses.

The Journey Through Grief is organized around the six needs that all mourners must yield to—indeed embrace—if they are to go on to find continued meaning in life and living. Following a short explanation of each mourning need is a series of brief, spiritual passages that, when read slowly and reflectively, help mourners work through their unique thoughts and feelings.

"The reflections in this book encourage you to think, yes, but to think with your heart and soul," writes Dr. Wolfelt. "They invite you to go to that spiritual place inside you and, transcending our mourning-avoiding society and even your own personal inhibitions about grief, enter deeply into the journey."

Now in softcover, this lovely book is more helpful (and affordable) than ever!

ISBN 1-879651-34-3 • 176 pages • softcover • $16.95
(plus additional shipping and handling)

Companion
PRESS

All Dr. Wolfelt's publications can be ordered by mail from:
Companion Press
3735 Broken Bow Road • Fort Collins, CO 80526
(970) 226-6050 • Fax 1-800-922-6051
www.centerforloss.com